T0354848

Thoughts From God For You

Kay Ashwell

WESTBOW
PRESS°
A DIVISION OF THOMAS NELSON
& ZONDERVAN

WestBow Press books may be ordered through booksellers or by contacting:

WestBow Press
A Division of Thomas Nelson & Zondervan
1663 Liberty Drive
Bloomington, IN 47403
www.westbowpress.com
844-714-3454

Scriptures taken from the Holy Bible, New International Version®, NIV®. Copyright © 1973, 1978, 1984, 2011 by Biblica, Inc.™ Used by permission of Zondervan. All rights reserved worldwide. www.zondervan.com The "NIV" and "New International Version" are trademarks registered in the United States Patent and Trademark Office by Biblica, Inc.®

ISBN: 978-1-6642-1057-8 (sc)
ISBN: 978-1-6642-1058-5 (hc)
ISBN: 978-1-6642-1056-1 (e)

Library of Congress Control Number: 2020921350

Print information available on the last page.

WestBow Press rev. date: 11/16/2020

Contents

Dedication

This book is dedicated to the memory of my loving husband Don. He struggled with understanding the love of God and my total love for him. After a time he began to understand these things. In the last months of his life he sang gospel songs and talked to God many times a day.

To Kevin Wirth who not only helped take care of Don the last five months of his life, showing patience and caring. Kevin, when not caring for Don, also helped me get this book ready for print.

It is also dedicated to all those who struggle with understanding Scripture and dealing with things in their life.

Permissions

Every Scripture used in this book are taken from the NIV Study Bible. Zondervan, 2008 update.

Prayer in the introduction is my own.

Bruce Wilkinson has written two books which have influenced my life in the past 20 years. 'The Prayer of Jabez' which encouraged me to pray the prayer and influenced me to carry out the things I believe God has instructed me to do. I have 3 thoughts on the prayer in these thoughts, but to my knowledge I have not copied any part of the book. It has influenced me in the way I teach. The other one that has encouraged me is 'Secrets of the Vine'.

Star Spangled Banner, poem written while he was watching the defense of Fort M'Henry on Sept. 14, 1814. Later set to music and became National Anthem of US. It is in the public domain.

O little Town of Bethlehem, copyright in Public Domain #121 on Public Domain Hymns to Glory to God.

Hark the Harold Angels, copyright in Public Domain #119 on Public Domain Hymns to Glory of God.

O' Come, O' Come Immanuel, written originally as a poem in the 12 Century, in the Public Domain for Advent.

Dictionary used is Webster's New World Dictionary of the American Language a Warner Books edition. Copyright 1984,1979, 1877, 1975, 1973, 1971 by Simon & Schuster, Inc.

Introduction

As I started this book I realized I was going to need to write an introduction. I also realized I would have to explain many things about myself and what has led me to write a book. I have a very hard time talking about myself at anytime but to put it into the public eye has been a new experience for me. All Scriptures used are from the NIV study Bible.

I have been a Christian since I was 12 years old. I had, as many do, built a wall around myself in self-defense and insecurity of being the oldest child. I had wonderful parents, but as the oldest, I felt responsible for many things and didn't feel like I should take their time away from the other kids to listen to my problems, so I built a wall of self-protection.

After I accepted the Lord into my life He started showing me His mercy, grace and peace. I was able to start letting the wall of protection down. It was as if I could see it disappearing a little at a time as I was able to understand why I had built it to start with. One day it was no longer there in front of me. He also showed me how to accept and handle the circumstances in my life.

As I became more sure that God was with me I started praying that I learn to love the way God loves. I prayed, 'Lord teach me to love the way you love', for years. I believe He has given me that love and the ability to accept people just where they are and He has also given me the desire to show that love to others. As time passed I came to understand that I wanted others to have the peace I felt from knowing my Father in Heaven. I began to teach Bible studies which later became the beginnings of three churches, each several years apart. All the while my Heavenly Father kept giving me more incite into understanding Scripture.

At the present time, in my 79 years, Christ has been a very active part of my life. He has given me knowledge that could have come only from

Him. He has been in control of my life and what I do since I was a teen. He has helped me through many negative situations in my life. He has given me a very positive attitude about life, and how to assist others through situations in their lives.

I believe He has been directing me to write this book for several years. In order to do that I have to tell you what and how He has been there for me all these years. My prayer is it will help others find the comfort and peace He has given me.

It is my firm belief that lessons we have learned are meant to be shared, as difficult as that is for some. I have learned many lessons, had several negative experiences, and had four major surgeries in my life. Through all four of them I have either felt him holding my hand or holding me in His arms. There has never been any fear of what was happening or in going through the surgeries. I always knew my Savior was there with me.

Although in my earlier years as a Christian I didn't understand all the ways He cared for me. I always felt His peace and the fact that He was showing me how to deal with them, and what He wanted me to learn and understand. He has also given me wisdom and understanding through the years.

My own thankfulness to my Lord: Father, You have been faithful all my life, even when I strayed for a short while. During those years which I allowed the world to guide me you were never far away. You were just waiting for me to open that door you were knocking on. Even then I knew you were with me and I never forgot who you were and who was calling me back. I can now see how you were working in my life and I learned what your plan was for me. I know you allowed me to be in the world for a time so I could understand how deceitful it is. You were preparing me to be able to follow your plan for me. I soon learned the world and what it offers had nothing to offer me. Since that time I have tried each day to be the person you desire me to be. It became clear to me you had called me to be a teacher. You have continued to give me the knowledge to understand Scripture and to be able to share that knowledge with others. Thank you Father. Amen.

There have been several times when I know for certain He has saved my life; the time I was a passenger in a car that went across several railroad tracks under the warning light. I looked up and that engine was close enough to touch, but somehow we made it over the tracks. Then there was the time I should have been hit head-on by a car passing a loaded semi on an S curve; the road was a very narrow 2 lane road with no edges, just ditches. The semi and I were just reaching each other, when the other car came around the semi, I could see the expression of fear on the semi driver's face, when all of a sudden my car went sideways onto a drive way and come to a stop. The other car passed the semi with the three of us abreast. I know I never could have done what happened without help, there was no time for me to react. It had to be the Lord. There is no other explanation for what happened.

God has given me the patience and understanding to raise my four children, four step children and two neighbor kids. Seven of them were teens. I have been given specific instructions over the years and learned patience, which comes from love, His love first.

When I had my hip replaced a number of years ago, He used me in a way I never would have imagined; but one that encouraged many people. It was what would become this book.

I was not able to be comfortable in bed for a time after I returned home from a rehab facility. I slept in my recliner several nights, I was only able to sleep two to three hours at a time. I remember distinctly Jesus talking to me through all my sleep times. He was reassuring me I was going to be fine, He also gave me insight into several things and several situations going on with friends and the hurt they were experiencing and the church in general. I believe He was preparing me for my next assignment from Him. After a week or so of this I was totally exhausted. I'm the type of person who needs at least seven or eight hours of good sleep each night. My husband Don was going to work one night, he was a gate keeper for a secured housing development, and I decided it would be a good time to try and figure out how to sleep in bed. I had always slept on my right side, but that was the hip I had replaced. I got into bed, lay on my left side and said to Jesus; I love the fact that you have shown me so many things and taught me the meaning of many Scriptures these past few weeks, but I need eight hours of sleep. I looked at the clock it said 10 PM. I remember, to this day, of being in a mountain meadow with a huge oak tree in the middle of it, I sat under the tree resting and feeling a cool breeze, I felt Jesus was there with me but He never said a word. At about the time I woke up I remember hearing words, which I believe where from Him, The words were to the effect of, do you see those sheep over there? Feed my sheep. I woke up and looked at the clock and it said 6 AM, I had been asleep for exactly eight hours.

Those words kept ringing in my ears, and about three days later I said to Him, Lord how am I supposed to feed your sheep? What do you want me to do? The very next day I awoke at 5 AM, went to the computer and started typing what came into my mind. A very encouraging thought came and when that thought was finished I felt I should send it to a few people by e-mail, those people were the ones who had been on my mind the last few weeks. Almost every morning from that day on I woke up at 5 AM and a new thought would come into my head. I would type it and send it. I didn't save the first few I wrote; then one day I felt I should be saving them.

Sometimes a new person would come to mind and I would add them to the list of those who received the daily thoughts. I never knew what the thoughts would be until I sat down each morning at the computor. There was never any preparation of what was said. I never read them after I sent them but started getting messages back about how that thought had helped them that day; sometimes they would tell me they had forwarded it on to someone they knew who needed that message. This situation continued every morning for about one and half years. I had thought several times I would quit writing them, but the thought was there every day. When I would think I was not going to send anymore, I would receive a note from someone who had received a thought saying how the messages had helped them through a very rough situation. One morning I awoke and the message was not there. Some asked why I quit writing them. At the same time when the thoughts stopped, we had a pastoral change and I took on the job of Education director and teaching the adult Sunday School Class at my church. I had also taken on a part time job as a cashier at the local Wal-Mart store; Don had to give his job up about a year before.

You will notice as you go through the readings they don't follow any set pattern. They have been randomly picked out of the over 400 written. If there were consecutive writings on a specific topic they will follow in order; The Jabez prayer, the warnings in Hebrews, and the Advent series, which starts after the thought 'God our anchor', and runs consecutively through Christmas day.

I have never written anything but my Sunday School Class lessons. I researched them each week in preparation for teaching on Sunday. I also kept getting led to research other things like the book of Revelation. After awhile I started teaching Wednesday evening services on Revelation. This idea of putting together a book of the daily thoughts kept nagging me. I have written hundreds of lessons for Sunday school since then and put together a daily devotional booklet for Advent, which was given to each family in the church to use, at home, during Advent. Still I felt I was being directed to write this book.

My husband, Don, started showing signs of Dementia about five years ago and four years ago I was diagnosed with a rare cancer, Adenoid Cystic Carcinoma. I had to have surgery and seven weeks of radiation treatments. Don's Dementia got worse. It was getting to the point I knew I needed to move us closer to the children; we had spent the last 12 years in a small town in Texas, both serving our Lord in a small church. I needed to stay in touch with my cancer doctor for awhile as follow-up, but three years ago I quit my job and made plans to bring us back to North Idaho near the children. We arrived in Idaho in May 2018.

At this time, I have Don at our home near the children. An attack he had in October of 2019 left him virtually bedridden. I am caring for him at our home. I have help getting him up, cleaned and dressed for the day and again in the evening preparing him and getting him into bed. I have no idea how long I will have him with me, but will care for him at home for the duration. I know one morning I will wake up and Jesus will have called him home. He loves to listen to gospel music and will sing along with the ones he knows. He also talks to Jesus several times a day.

The man who has helped me with caring for Don the past five months is a Christian, he has been writing and editing books and encouraged me to put this book together. A few months before he came to us he felt he was to move from the state he was living in to this area of Idaho. He followed that feeling and Don was the first person he had been given to assist caring for. You can call that coincidence, I call it Gods direction.

Today March 14, 2020 at 8:35 AM Jesus called my husband Don Home to be with Him. Yet another time God has given me the peace, love, and strength to get through another trial. I know he is with me always. Even though you know death is coming, you are never prepared for when it does.

I don't know what lies ahead, but God does and I know He will see me through whatever comes. This book only holds just over 100 of those daily thoughts. Perhaps there will be a second book with more of them; or something else altogether, whatever is ahead I know God will direct me and give me the wisdom and strength to get through it and follow His leading. I never walk alone; my Lord is always with me.

As I have read these thoughts for the first time, I find a theme throughout; I believe there are warnings in the messages for everyone, everywhere. There are four types of people and there are four types of growth. Those who will never come to Him; those who will start believing and then find it easier to follow the ways of the world, but like to make others think they are sincere; then there are those who believe and try to follow Him, but for one reason or another didn't follow up on learning His ways; and then there are those who have stepped up and continue to carry the light of God to others because they have found He can sustain them every day through whatever comes along.

> Revelations 3:13-16. "I know your deeds, that you are neither cold nor hot. I wish you were either one or the other; so, because you are lukewarm-neither hot nor cold – I am about to spit you out of my mouth."

Christians are God's Church, we are His people, those just playing at being one of His are getting a very clear message. It's time to get hot in your walk of faith.

Those who do not call the Lord their Father need to make that decision soon, time is getting shorter by the day.

My prayer is that when this book gets published and the people who read it will be given new insight to my Jesus. They will come to know Him as Savior and be able to feel His peace, love, mercy, joy and hope which I have felt for most of my life.

God bless each of you who read this book.

Kay Ashwell

Anchor

God Our Anchor

Good morning:

A blue sky and sunshine brings renewed hope. The earth is renewed from the rain. As I write this thought some would say our country has new hope. Regardless of what you expected or wanted from the 2012 election, which has just been held, one thing is sure; it will bring about some sort of change. Good or bad no one knows at this point. But one thing we know for sure as Christians our God never changes. The promises He has made He will keep.

> Hebrews 6:17-20a; "Because God wanted to make the unchanging nature of His purpose very clear to the heirs of what was promised, He confirmed it with an oath. God did this so that, by two unchangeable things in which it is impossible for God to lie; we who have fled to take hold of the hope offered to us may be greatly encouraged. We have this hope as an anchor for the soul, firm and secure. It enters the inner sanctuary behind the curtain, where Jesus, who went before us, has entered on our behalf".

Unlike the world and governments, our God is unchangeable. We can depend on Him to be here for us whenever we are in need and come to Him. It says He is an anchor for our soul. An anchor in a ship or boat holds it firm and steady, that's what God does for us when we stand firm on His promises. He holds us firm and strong. Ready to deal with anything our enemy throws at us. We just have to claim the promises and obey the directions He is giving us.

This is sort of a second thought, but not entirely separate. When I think of our country, as I have the past couple of days, with all the election news; I am reminded when I look out front and see our flag gently flying in the breeze, how firm our men and women have stood in their hope of keeping freedom alive.

They are unwavering in their duty, and in their love of country. When I look at our flag I always think of 'The Star Spangled Banner'. Most of us know it, but sadly many of our children and grandchildren don't know the words of the first stanza. There are other stanzas which are not as well known by most.

"Oh, say, can you see, by the dawn's early light, what so proudly we hailed at the twilight's last gleaming...The Star Spangled Banner in triumph shall wave o'er the land of the free and the home of the brave!" This is just part of the first verse.

We may be in a war zone all day, but we go home to a safe haven knowing that our God has been there with us. Then we realize we may only have a few hours of rest before it starts all over again. Always remember, God is always on the throne, just as our service men and women are always on guard of our freedoms.

The other verse of the song, which I love and which I wish we all knew,

"Praise the Power that hath made and preserved us a nation! Then conquer we must, when our cause it is just, and this be our motto, in God is our trust."

Yes, God is our trust, our redeemer, and our hope for the future; not only for us and an eternal home with Him, but for our nation which is an anchor for the rest of the world. When you pray; always remember our service men and women and our country. It needs to stand firm in these unchanging times. Just as we need to stand firm in our love for our God and the promises we have in Him. He is our anchor in this world.

Have a great day and God bless!

Advent

Advent and Preparation

Good morning:

Tomorrow starts the Advent Season! This has been a special time in my life since I was a young girl. We would always have our manger scene up and the advent wreath ready. Some may not know what Advent is. The word advent comes from Latin meaning "come" and refers to Jesus coming into our world. It starts four Sundays prior to Christmas Day. The Festival of Christmas wasn't established until the fourth century. Advent was originally 40 days long. It represented the four thousand years of patient waiting, on the part of the Hebrews, for the promised Messiah.

The meaning of Advent is the longing for deliverance from oppression along with the anticipation of the Messiah. It is a time of prayer, not of fasting as some think. It is a time to be centering on God who gave us His son Jesus, who is the King of Grace.

The Advent wreath is very symbolic of Christ and the purpose for using one is to deepen our understanding of Christmas. Some of you may be saying to yourself, I know the meaning of Christmas and the coming of our Lord. That may be true, but there is nothing like focusing on it every day prior to His birth, you will begin to anticipate His coming. I hope all of you join me today and every day this advent season. Make your Advent wreath today and be ready to light a candle each day with me.

The base of the wreath is round and covered with greens. The circular base represents life without end, eternal life. It is also a symbol of God's unending love for each of us. The green which covers the base represents the continuation of a life lived in Christ. There are five candles, three purple or violet, one pink and one white. The purple candles are lit the first, second, and fourth weeks; they symbolize our *penitence* and *preparation*. The pink candle lit on the third week is to symbolize our *joy*. In the center is the white candle symbolizing Christ as the center of our life. (If you can't find purple candies you can use red in their place.)

Now you are ready to light the candle of the week each day and have a time of devotion in your home. It doesn't matter if you are single, a couple, or a whole family. Set aside time each day to light the candle, have the daily devotion, and pray. My children grew up with it and some still use it in their homes each year. It is a good tradition to start if you don't already do it. Each day from tomorrow through Christmas Day I am going to give you a scripture and devotional focus for the day.

I pray this will be a blessing to you the next four weeks as we look expectantly to the coming of our Savior and King. This will be a very busy time in most of our lives, but take time to focus on our Lord and the meaning of this season. If you are alone you will be drawn even closer to the one who is keeping you now in his loving hands. If you are a couple this special time each day will not only draw you closer to the Lord, but it will draw you closer to each other. If you are a family it will draw the family closer together as you take time to share and become united together in the bond of love which is given by our Lord and the children will gain a sense of expectancy of His birth and understand what the Christmas season is all about; a lasting impression for life, not just on what presents they get.

Another thing I did with my children was to have them pick someone who would not have any gifts for Christmas; they would get them a gift and give it to them just prior to Christmas Day. It had to be someone who they would not receive anything from. This taught them the reason for giving; it also taught them what was given to us by God as a baby is a living gift of love.

Have a great day and God bless!

Advent Week 1 Day 1

Good morning:

This is the first day of Advent, a time of preparation for the coming of our Lord and Savior. As Christmas approaches, take comfort and be glad, for once again the Long-awaited One stands at our door! Let us prepare our hearts and home to greet our Lord.

Light the first purple or violet (or red) candle it is the Prophesy Candle. It calls us to Immanuel!

Prepare for the coming event; it reminds us of the prophets of the Old Testament who foretold the coming of the Messiah, Jesus, who would bring peace and love and salvation to the world.

> John 8: 12, "I am the light of the world. Whoever follows me will never walk in darkness, but will have the light of life".

Our first scripture reading is from Isaiah, 9: 2, 6~7. Isaiah was a prophet sent by God, about 750 years before the birth of Christ. He was sent to warn the people of Israel about many things including their need to prepare for the coming of the Messiah. The people of Israel were living in darkness; much like the world today is living in darkness. They had a hope that the Messiah would come and bring light to their miserable existence. Jesus did that, He became the light of the world. Never again will people need to live in darkness and despair!

Even though we have the scriptures to tell us how to live in the light and how to have *peace* and *joy* in our hearts, there is a world around us that is still living in darkness. There are people who are still living without the hope of the gospel. They are living in hopelessness.

We have been given the light; let it shine so others can see it. Pray during this holiday season that God will use you to help spread the light to a world that cannot see. For us, the world is our family, our neighbors, our community and beyond.

> Isaiah 9:2; "The people walking in darkness have seen a great light; on those living in the land of the shadow of death a light has dawned."

That is talking about us, Christians, we once walked in darkness, and then God had mercy on us and showed us the light. We no longer have to walk in the shadow of darkness; we have been given the light of God.

> Isaiah 2:6; "For to us a child is born, to us a son is given, and the government will be on his shoulders. And he will be called Wonderful, Counselor, Mighty God, Everlasting Father, and Prince of Peace."

What beautiful names we have been given for Christ. Dwell on these names; He is with us giving us help on how to walk our life with Him.

Mighty God! We only have to look around us to see the mighty hand of God in creation.

Everlasting Father! He is always there for us through eternity.

Prince of Peace! when we walk with Him we have the peace He gives us in knowing He is taking care of us. These are promises to us. Remember these names and the promises as you go forward.

> Isaiah 2:7, "Of the increase of His government and peace there will be no end. He will reign on David's throne and over His kingdom, establishing and upholding it with justice and righteousness from that time on and forever. The zeal of the Lord Almighty will accomplish this."

Kay Ashwell

This is the promise that Jesus will come from the lineage of King David, He will reign over His kingdom, the one to come, with righteousness forever. The zeal, with which He will reign, is like a jealous lover, who will not abandon His people.

Let us keep these promises in our hearts and minds as we walk toward our goal of eternity with Him. We need not fear, Our Savior is taking care of us. We just have to be willing to let Him. We have a job to do for Him. Pray today that He will have control of every little piece of your life. Then let others, especially family, know that Jesus loves them too and wants to live with them also. Live in the comfort of Isaiah 2: 6.

Have a great day and God bless!

Advent Week 1 Day 2

Good Morning:

Today we light our Prophecy candle and read:

> Isaiah 61:1~4; "The Spirit of the Sovereign Lord is on me, because the Lord has anointed me to preach good news to the poor. He has sent me to bind up the brokenhearted, to proclaim freedom for the captives, and release from darkness for the prisoners, to proclaim the year of the Lord's favor, and the day of vengeance of our God, to comfort all who mourn, and provide for those who grieve in Zion to bestow on them a crown of beauty instead of ashes; the oil of gladness instead of mourning; and a garment of praise instead of a spirit of despair. They will be called oaks of righteousness, a planting of the Lord for the display of his splendor. They will rebuild the ancient ruins and restore the places long devastated, they will renew the ruined cities that have been devastated for generations."

Israel is the nation of people God has chosen for His kingdom. Once you have received the mercy of God and have become one of His children you are now a part of the nation of Israel. The words we just read from Isaiah are also the words spoken by Jesus at the synagogue in Nazareth when He started His ministry. (Luke 4: 16~21)

Through His life and ministry, Jesus fulfilled the words of the wonderful prophecy: God's Spirit was on Him, he preached good tidings, healed the broken-hearted, proclaimed liberty to the captives, and opened the prisons of those who were bound. Today we are fortunate because Jesus continues to perform these same roles in our lives. The scriptures teach of His good news. He draws us ever closer to Himself. He heals the broken hearted; many of us who have suffered or are suffering from fractures of the heart have found this promise to be true. He proclaims freedom for those who are caught in sin; through Him we can experience freedom from these addictions and sins which control us. He continues to call the lonely, the hurt, and the persecuted to Himself. We can find comfort in His promises. We can find shelter in the time of storms in His loving arms. He is our Counselor, our Redeemer, and our Prince of Peace.

> Isaiah 41:10 & 13, "So do not fear, for I am with you, do not be dismayed, for I am your God. I will strengthen you and help you; I will uphold you with my righteous right hand...13, For I am the Lord, your God who takes hold of your right hand and says to you, do not fear; I will help you."

Sometimes the fears we have are imagined, and sometimes they are real. Sometimes we are caught in situations over which we have no control, and sometimes we cause those situations ourselves. But God's word to Israel and to us is the same; do not fear! I will help you. This is the promise we hold onto as we look expectantly toward Christmas.

Isaiah reminds us of who Jesus is and what He will do for us if we only let Him. He came and still comes to set us free from the sins of this world.

> Galatians 5:1 says, "It is for freedom that Christ has set us free. Stand firm then, and do not let yourselves be burdened again by a yoke of slavery (sin)."

As we move ever closer to Christmas these and other promises from God should comfort us and give us the joy and peace that can only come from knowing and serving Jesus. Look with anticipation to what He has in store for your life and be glad He is in control. Keep your minds and hearts in touch with Him as we look expectantly to His coming.

Have a great day and God bless!

Advent Week 1, Day 3

Good morning:

As you light the Prophecy candle today and read:

> Isaiah 40:1-8. "Comfort, my people," says your God. Verse 3-4, "A voice of one calling in the desert prepare the way for the Lord, make straight in the wilderness a highway for our God. Every valley shall be raised up, every mountain and hill made low; the rough ground shall become level. The rugged places a plain. And the glory of the Lord will be revealed, and all mankind together will see it, for the mouth of the Lord has spoken."

What a glorious passage! It refers to the coming of a King. In Biblical times, before a King would come everyone would prepare for his arrival. Everything was cleaned, refurbished, painted, and even crooked roads were straightened and fixed. Are we preparing for the arrival of our King?

The theme of this week is *Prepare*. In the middle of the hustle and bustle of Christmas we need to stop long enough to open our hearts to Jesus. We should not give Him the leftovers, but should focus our attention upon His coming. What a tragedy, if we spend, spend, spend, and find that it was all for nothing, that we were in such a frenzy that we missed the real point and the great joy and contentment of Christmas.

In my younger years, I would make sure that the gifts to be given were purchased or made prior to the beginning of Advent, then I could spend time preparing the cards and greetings I was sending out. I would have time every evening to read and talk about Jesus' coming birth with my children. They still remember the times we spent together making cookies, candies, listening to Christmas carols, reading the Christmas

Kay Ashwell

and winter stories. I haven't had any little ones around at Christmas time for several years, but I still like to read the Christmas story, listen to Christmas music and my heart is still filled with joy and memories.

We have to prepare for the Lord's coming, especially His second coming. What are you doing to prepare for Jesus' coming? Are you ready if He should come today? We need to be in communion with Him. We need to be looking forward, for Him. This means we need to be searching for Him, reaching for Him, anticipating His arrival. Our hearts need to be pure and clean.

There was a man in the temple in Jerusalem that was looking for Him. He was searching and looking forward to His arrival. That man was Simeon. He had been told by God that he would not die until he had seen the Messiah.

> Luke 2:21~39; verses 27~32, Moved by the Spirit, he went into the temple courts, "When the parents brought in the child Jesus, to do for Him what the custom of the Law required, Simeon took Him in his arms and praised God, saying; "Sovereign Lord, as you have promised, you now dismiss your servant to peace. For my eyes have seen your salvation which you have prepared in the sight of all people; a light for revelation to the Gentiles and for glory to your people Israel."

We were Gentiles until we accepted Christ as our Savior, then we became a part of the people of Israel.

Simeon was looking with anticipation for the Messiahs' arrival, are you looking with the same anticipation? Are you looking forward? Don't let the commercialization of Christmas take away the joy of this special time of year. Be prepared! Let others know you are prepared, let them see the preparation through your life!

Have a great day and God bless!

Advent Week 1 Day 4

Good morning:

Today is the fourth day of Advent. As we continue to prepare for Christmas we are continuing to read the Prophecy of the coming of our Lord. Today's scripture is found in Isaiah 7:14 and Matthew 1:23. They are exactly the same scripture, Isaiah foretold of Christ's coming.

> Isaiah 7:14, "Therefore the Lord Himself will give you a sign, the virgin will be with child and will give birth to a son, and will call His name Immanuel." In Matthew1:20 an angel has come to Joseph in a dream. Matthew 1: 23 "The virgin will be with child and will give birth to a son, and they will call him Immanuel because it means, "God with us."

Joseph and Mary were living in Nazareth when the angel came to them. Nazareth was a small country town, but out of it, came the greatest good the world has ever known. Nazareth therefore is a word suggesting God's grace. In a humble home in that town, God found a virgin in whom the divine Savior would be conceived by His Spirit. There the child would grow up, secure his education, learn a trade, declare his mission, and go forth.

As Christmas approaches we need to remember that we are a part of the nation of Israel and we need to understand the ancestry of our Lord and be proud of the fact that we are a part of that ancestry. We need to be excited to be a part of His family, we should be able to speak of Jesus and say, like Him, I am a child of the Most High God. We can call Jesus our brother and we can share with Him in the riches of God's kingdom, even though the evil one is trying to sell us into slavery.

Be careful of your thoughts, your actions, and where your mind is focused at this time. It is so easy to get caught up in all the commercial aspects of Christmas. We are told that we should call this a 'Winter Festival' so no one is offended. People say 'Happy Holidays' and it is very apparent that Christ is being left out. As a part of His family we must carry His name forward. It is up to us to greet people with a Merry Christmas; to display, through our actions and our voices that He is the 'Reason for the Season'. He needs to become more important in today's world than at any other time in history.

As we give this season to various organizations, and to friends and family, let us remember that all acts of giving should start with a complete submission to Jesus. We have to have Him first in our lives. Then the gifts we give will come from the heart and not for any other reason. If we give because we are expected to we are not in the right place with God and we need to come to grips with the fact that our heart is not in the right place. We should give because of the love which God has given to us, and because of the grace He so generously has given us. People need positives in their lives and this is the perfect time to show the *love* and *grace* of God. It is the perfect time to tell others about the Jesus who saved us from our sinful lives. It is the perfect time to be Jesus to the world.

Is your heart in the right place today? Are you willing to be Jesus to others? Are the gifts you are buying bought with a heart of love or because they are expected? We need to constantly evaluate where we are in our walk with the Lord. His love needs to shine forth in all we do and say.

Have a great day and God bless!

Advent Week 1 Day 5

Good morning;

As you light the candle today read Matthew 1:1-17. To many this will be a boring read, one in which you have a hard time pronouncing the names. You may wonder why Matthew would even put this in his story of Jesus. Matthew felt it was important for Jews of that day to understand Jesus' heritage. To the Jews of that day their heritage, their family name, was very important. It told who they were, how much they should be respected and who they were related to. Matthew felt the world should know that Jesus came from a long line of honored and respected men. That He truly was a Jew and came from the line of David, just as the prophets had foretold.

The genealogy in Matthew is a genealogy of a King. If you look at this passage closely you will see it is divided into three sections. This is symbolic of human life.

The first section tells the story and history up to David, which is greatness.

The second section takes the story up to the exile in Babylon and is a story of captivity, shame, tragedy and disaster.

The third section takes the story up to Jesus, where we find liberation from the captivity of sin. We find love, forgiveness, and grace.

It is interesting to note that these same three sections can tell us our spiritual history.

Section one tells us that we have been reborn into greatness. We were created in God's image. God's dream for us is for greatness.

Section two tells us about how our humanity has used its free will to defy and disobey God through our selfish desires and self-importance.

Kay Ashwell

Section three gives to us the knowledge that greatness can be regained. God did not give up on man, He sent His Son to redeem and rescue our lost lives.

All through the history in this scripture are stories of how God was always with His people, even when they did not know Him or ask Him to be with them. God always rescued His people, He always loved His people and He always redeemed them and brought them back to Himself. We can praise Him today for the lessons He has shown us. The lesson that He loves us; He wants the best for us. It shows us no matter what we get ourselves into, He will always be there to bring us out of it and back to Him.

Remember today, and each day during Advent and beyond, the provisions God has given us for salvation.

Remember the meaning of Christmas! Remember that the Son of God came to earth as a baby, learned the ways of man, walked through life to show us how to walk. He walked straight to the cross where He died to carry all the sin of the world to death. Then to show man how they could be lifted up again; He arose and became the risen Lord. This is the salvation message.

We are born into a sinful life, we walk in a sinful world and become sinful ourselves, but we have a chance to be redeemed. This redemption can only take place when we give our all to Him, when we surrender our will, or selfish desires, and our pride to Him. Then He will lift us up and call us His. We then become part of His genealogy, part of His family.

We need to praise Him for the grace He has given us. We need to thank Him for the love and tolerance He has for us, even when we don't do what He asks. He is always there waiting for us to ask Him in again. Our patience with people and situations should be no less than His is for us.

Remember this Christmas season the 'Reason for the Season' and from where it came, how it came and what it means for us.

God bless and have a great day!

Advent Week 1 Day 6

Good Morning:

As you light your candle this morning we are going to read Luke 1:46-55 keep in mind that Mary is probably only 13 or 14 years old. After she gets the news from God she prepares to go see Elisabeth, a cousin, who is married to Zechariah, a priest. Elisabeth is with child, the future John the Baptist. It is called Mary's Song.

> Luke 1:46-55; "My soul glorifies the Lord and my spirit rejoices in God my Savior, for He has been mindful of the humble state of His servant. From now on generations will call me blessed, For the Mighty One has done great things for me - holy is his name. His mercy extends to those who fear him, from generation to generation. He has performed mighty deeds with his arm; he has scattered those who are proud in their inmost thoughts. He has brought rulers down from their thrones but has lifted up the humble. He has filled the hungry with good things but has sent the rich away hungry. He has helped his servant Israel, remembering to be merciful to Abraham and his descendents forever, even as he said to our fathers.

There are some key words in this scripture, as you read it you will see favor and grace in what she is saying. Fear, in Scripture, is to revere God, not be afraid of Him. Mary is giving God praise and is thanking Him for His grace on the nation on Israel. The words, like favor and grace are not used but are words we would use today. Favor is found in the choice of Mary to bear the most precious of all heavenly gifts. Mary is in awe and humble at the honor given her. She doesn't feel worthy, yet knows the honor is a great one. Isaiah had foretold that a virgin would give birth to God's Son. But Mary never imagined it would come through her. She shows humility and honor in these passages.

Kay Ashwell

Grace is the message of the second half of these verses. It shows the grace given with the Messiah's coming. We should be humbled when we realize that God came to us in the form of an infant, to become human. Human, so we can understand it is possible to be separated from the world and made whole in Him. He came as a human to experience life, to give us knowledge, to know and feel what we experience in life. He knew He would be the sacrificial lamb, but wanted us to know that He had experienced life on earth, that He had a better life for us. He came to give us *hope* for the future. When He left He knew He had to give us the Spirit to carry us through; the Spirit would be His voice in us.

We have a savior who understands and knows our pressures, temptations, and trials. He understands what this world is like. He has a *peace* we all need to experience when we believe and follow His path. He is the provider of victory even in the middle of turmoil and an ungodly world. So as you read this passage keep all this in mind and rest in the fact that we have God's grace and favor as our guiding light.

Praise is to God, the Father, Son and Holy Spirit. Through them we can have hope for the coming of His kingdom. We can rest in the promises of God and look expectantly for His return. As we get ever closer to His birth, walk in His light, with His love toward others, with tolerance, and prayers for the lost of the world. Walk with a song in your heart and a smile on your face, our savior has promised to be with us through it all.

Have a great day and God bless!

Advent Week 1 Day 7

Good morning:

Today ends the first week of Advent and as it comes to an end, we have talked about how prophets of old foretold of God's free gift. Tomorrow we will start the second week of Advent and light the second candle, the Bethlehem Candle.

Today's scripture is Ephesians 2:1-14, which is to long to print but I suggest you read it. It is a beautiful scripture describing the wonderful gift of life God has given to us. It talks about the ruler of the kingdom of the air, which is Satan. It also talks about Gentiles not having been circumcised. This is difficult for some to understand. What it means is that before we accepted Christ as our savior, we were part of the Gentile world, we were sinners, but after we accepted Christ we were no longer a Gentile, we became part of His family, a Jew, with the same fully vested inheritance. God has circumcised us, in other words; He has taken out the sin and gotten rid of it, the same way we cut a bad spot out of something. God has given us new life. Please read this passage with new understanding.

We all think about gifts at Christmas, and we are as little kids come Christmas morning when we can unwrap those colorful gifts stacked under the tree. We need to be unwrapping the beautiful gift God has given us, the incomprehensible gift of *love* He gave to us in Christ Jesus. This gift is free to us, a gift we can unwrap each day of the year, just by asking Him each morning to walk with us through the day and thank Him at the end of each day for keeping us safe.

He has given us this gift, not because we deserve it, but because He loves us so much. God's desire is to bring all things in heaven and on earth together under one head, Christ Jesus.

God provided the people of Israel with many hints about how, where, and when Jesus would be born. He gave them everything they needed to recognize the Messiah so they could believe and follow Him. They didn't understand.

God has provided us with many hints and instructions as well. He has given us all the information we need to live holy and unselfish lives. Do we live that way? Do we search the scriptures daily until we know them by heart? When we have found them do we follow them? Do we follow the example He has given us in Jesus? Do we love others more than we love ourselves? That is the *miracle of Christmas;* to love as much as God loved when He gave the world His only Son.

Advent is the perfect time to begin a habit of spending time in the word every day, even if it is only a verse or two. It is a perfect time to spend time with Him, talking to Him. It is the perfect time to start loving the way He loves by acting unselfishly toward others. Ask Him to show you how to love the way He loves, you will be surprised how you change when you ask that each day.

As a Christian we have already reached out and accepted God's free gift. We have been given the instructions of how to live. We need to thank Him for this lavish gift. If you haven't yet accepted Him into your life, this is the perfect time to do so. You only have to ask, with a sincere heart, for your sins to be forgiven, ask Him to lead you from now on into His ways and then accept the free gift He offers you.

We all need to start showing this free gift to others, through a kind word, a friendly greeting, a smile, then see how much joy we receive. See how much easier our day goes. Give others the free gift of love that God has given us.

> Ephesians 2:13-14 "But now in Christ Jesus, you who once were far away having been bought near through the blood of Christ. For He Himself is our peace, who has made the two one and has destroyed the barrier, the dividing wall of hostility".

Have a great day and God bless!

Advent Week 2 Day 1

Good morning:

Today we begin the second week of Advent. We will light the first purple candle, the Prophecy Candle, and then light the second purple candle, the Bethlehem Candle. This Bethlehem Candle reminds us that Christ was born as a human baby, in a specific place, and a specific time in history. This is called 'Incarnation', which means born in human form. This is one of the beautiful mysteries of Christmas. That Jesus was born both God and Man. Jesus the man, Christ the God. This second candle is also the Hope Candle, because Jesus is our *hope*.

The song, O Little Town of Bethlehem, is one of the popular Christmas songs of the church. It was written in 1868 by Phillip Brooks. I particularly think verses 3 & 4 are beautiful. They tell the beautiful reason Jesus was sent to us.

How silently, how silently,
The wondrous gift is given!
So God imparts to human hearts,
The blessing of His heaven.
No ear may hear His coming,
But in this world of sin,
Where meek souls will receive Him still,
The dear Christ enters in.

O holy Child of Bethlehem,
Descend to us, we pray;
Cast out our sin and enter in,
Be born in us today.
We hear the Christmas angels
The great glad tidings tell;
O come to us, abide in us,
Our Lord Immanuel.

Kay Ashwell

Remember we discovered last week that Immanuel means 'God with us'. Today's scripture verses are found in Micah 5:2 and Matthew 2:1-6. It is in these verses that scripture tells us where Christ is to be born.

> Micah 5: 2; "But you, Bethlehem Ephrathah, though you are small among the clans of Judah, out of you will come for me one who will be ruler over Israel, whose origins are from of old, from ancient times"

In this passage you will find the word Ephrathah, it is just telling us the geographical region of Bethlehem.

> Matthew 2:6, "But you, Bethlehem, in the land of Judah, are by no means lost among the rulers of Judah; for out of you will come a ruler who will be the shepherd of my people Israel."

Bethlehem has a long history in scripture, it is where Jacob buried Rachel and where Ruth lived and married Boaz. But above all it was the home of King David. It was through the line of David that Jesus was to be born. The people of that day expected Jesus to be a king that would lead them out of bondage. Instead He was born a baby, an infant that needed to be cared for. Bethlehem is a small, quiet town and in the poor section of town, in a stable the baby was born. This is important because He was coming to save the poor, the down in spirit, the ones with no hope.

God sent His son to a significant place to be born into a poor family; for the entire world, a world full of lost humanity. He wasn't just sent for the wealthy or the beautiful, He was sent for all mankind. Even though the Jews of Jesus day knew the scriptures they were not prepared for His arrival. It is hard for us to understand as well, because if the scholars of that day had understood it would have meant they would have to change everything they taught and had been taught. It is the same today, when we accept Christ we have to change, how we think, how we speak, how we act.

The world doesn't want to change, have you changed? Are you ready to receive Christ? It means making changes, but the wonderful thing is He will be with you to help make the changes in your life. He will never leave you on your own. You just have to ask Him every day to help you, to be with you.

As we begin this week let us remember, O come to us, abide in us, Our Lord Immanuel.

Have a great day and God bless!

Advent Week 2 Day 2

Good morning:

This morning as we light both the Prophecy and the Bethlehem Candles reflect back on the past week. Have you moved forward in your walk with God or have you remained the same? Yesterday we lit the second candle, The Bethlehem or Hope Candle and found out that our Lord was to be born in Bethlehem; a town that had been the home of several of God's people from ancient times. The word Bethlehem means The House of Bread. It stood in an area of the land which was fertile. It was well known as an area of farming and the growing of wheat. The story of Ruth gives us insight into this and also the true meaning of love. If you are not familiar with the story of Ruth, read the Book of Ruth in the Old Testament, it is not long.

So the town of Bethlehem was to be the birth place of our Lord and Savior. How fitting, Jesus is our Bread of Life. The sad thing is the world does not understand this. The world today is too busy, it scurry's about looking for ways to feed, clothe, house, and entertain the body, when it is the soul that needs feeding.

Jesus, The Bread of Life; John 6:25-59, is our scripture today, it is very long, but you need to get your Bible and read it. Jesus is telling the people that they must eat of the bread of life and that He is that bread of life. Many miss the point of what Jesus is saying in these verses, just as the people of that day missed the fact of Him being the Messiah. He is telling us that we must eat the nourishment of His word and drink from His cup of life, through His death on the cross for the sinful world. We must seek The Bread of Life because He came to sustain, satisfy, and nourish our lives.

God sent His only Son into this world so we could know how much He loved His creation, man. So we could know Him through His Son, Jesus. He sent Jesus into the world to show it how to have eternal life; which has to come through Jesus. Yet, the world and many so called Christians have missed the fact that eternal life is the gift of Christ.

To achieve eternal life is not in what we do, not by how much we work in the church, not how much we can tithe to the church; it is in the simple fact that we believe in God's son, Jesus Christ. We believe in His birth, His message of love and His death, which He freely gave, and in His resurrection, the power to overcome death.

Jesus is the free gift given to us. He only asks that we hear his message of love and allow Him to work through our lives. We must be in the word, be in prayer and He will lead us in the path He has chosen for our lives, and that we accept His gift of death on the cross so we can have a way to eternal life with Him.

He is our *bread of life,* all things come from Him and through Him. We can continue to battle the world each day or we can choose to follow the path He leads us in. It won't be a bed of roses, He didn't promise that, but He did promise that He would be there with us, to help us all along the way.

> John 6: 37-40; "All that the Father gives me will come to me, and whoever comes to me I will never drive away. For I have come down from heaven not to do my will but to do the will of Him who sent me; And this is the will of Him who sent me, that I shall lose none of all that He has given me, but raise them up at the last day. For my Father's will is that everyone who looks to the Son and believes in Him shall have eternal life, and I will raise him up at the last day."

How long has it been since you ate from the Bread of Life? How long will it be before you let Him nourish your soul? Let this Advent season be the time you get back into the word, back into a time of prayer with Him. Let Him nourish you and give you the *hope* that is in Christmas.

The Bethlehem Candle represents the *hope* of life in Christ.

Have a great day and God bless!

Kay Ashwell

Advent Week 2 Day 3

Good morning:

Today we read about the birth of Jesus. The very familiar story:

> Luke 2:1-7; "In those days Caesar Augustus issued a decree that a census should be taken of the entire Roman world. (This was the first census taken while Quirinius was governor of Syria.) And everyone went to his own town to register. So Joseph also went up from the town of Nazareth in Galilee to Judea, to Bethlehem the town of David, because he belonged to the house and line of David. He went there to register with Mary, who was pledged to be married to him and was expecting a child. While they were there the time came for the baby to be born, and she gave birth to her firstborn, a son. She wrapped him in cloths and placed him in a manger, because there was no room for them in the inn".

There are some facts I want to bring out from these verses. First we see that an exact time in history has been given to this story. Luke tells us that it was during the reign of Caesar Augustus and that Quirinius was governor of Syria. There has always been debate about the date, but one fact is clear, in all scripture it was during the time of Caesar Augustus. He was the first Roman Emperor having replaced the republic with an imperial form of government. He expanded the empire to include the entire Mediterranean world. Since it was the custom to have a census taken, it seems feasible that a census was ordered to see how many people this incorporated and how much could be collected in taxes.

Since Joseph was from the line of David, and we learned last week that Bethlehem was the home of David. Joseph had to return to the birth place of his ancestors. Mary was due to give birth at anytime so this was a particularly difficult time for her. Bethlehem was approximately

75 miles from Nazareth and it took at least 3 days to travel there. Even riding on a donkey, the journey had to be extremely difficult for her.

Jesus was born in a stable, or a cave as they were often used to house animals and there is a cave in the city of Bethlehem. It says because there was no room for them at the inn. I believe the place of His birth is significant. He was sent into the world to save the world. Scripture refers to Him as having no home of His own, no place to lay His head. He called men, who were considered the poorest at the time, to be His disciples. He healed the sick, including lepers who were outcasts. He spent time with those who were disliked and even called a tax collector to be a disciple. So to be born in a stable, fit only for animals, to me is a significant factor about who He was. He came to show the truth and give hope to the downtrodden of the world. The wealthy have their reward on earth; those who believe in Him will receive their reward in the eternal life to come.

The birth of Christ is the focal point of Christmas and the center of the Christian's faith. We already know we belong to Him and are a part of His family as Christians.

> Hebrews 2:11-13, "Both the one who makes men holy and those who are made holy" are of the same family. So Jesus is not ashamed to call us bothers. He says, 'I will declare your name to my brothers; in the presence of the congregation I will sing your praises. And again, I will put my trust in Him. And again he says, here I am, and with the children God has given me."

This can be compared to Psalm 22:22-28, which speaks of praise to the Lord. It describes the expanding company of those who will take up the praise. No psalm or prophecy contains a greater vision of the scope of the throng of worshipers who will join in the praise of God's saving acts.

This Christmas season declare that Jesus is your brother, love Him, respect Him, allow Him to help you overcome your trials and troubles by giving them to Him to handle. He came as a human baby to identify

Himself with humans and with His sacrifice on the cross to restore our lost holiness.

We have challenges facing us every day. Many of us don't have fancy homes or new cars, but we do have *peace* that is beyond our understanding. This is because He takes us through life's challenges and helps us achieve the goals He has set for us. Goals we have no idea how to achieve on our own.

As we near the day of His birth give your all to Him, give your worries to Him. He will help you carry the load the world has put on you so that others can see through your actions that they can also receive peace also.

Have a great day and God bless!

Advent Week 2 Day 4

Good morning:

Today's scripture is Matthew 2:1-12. This is too long a Scripture to copy, so please read it. This is the story of the Magi coming to worship the King of the Jews. It is assumed that they were Astrologers, with some religious interest, from the east. We do not know where in the east, but possibly from Persia or southern Arabia. This is a fascinating part of the birth story that has caused a lot of speculation. They observed a strange star in the sky and decided it was a significant royal birth. It is assumed there were three of them because of the mention of the three gifts, but scripture does not tell us how many made the journey.

They believed Jesus was born a king, so it was natural for them to go to Jerusalem, the center of Judea. Since they believed this was a royal birth they naturally went to the palace of the king of Judea, who at that time was Herod. Herod was a non Jew who had been appointed by the Roman ruler. He was ruthless, murdering anyone including a wife, three sons, a mother-in-law, and uncles, who posed a threat to his power.

Contrary to the portrayal of the birth which we are all familiar with, the Magi didn't see Jesus the night of His birth. They arrived about two years after the first sighting of the star. Our scripture today relates to the meeting with Herod and the wise men. They were advised that the child was probably in Bethlehem as the prophets had written.

The chief priests mentioned in these verses were the Sadducees, who were in charge of worship at the temple in Jerusalem, teachers of the Jewish law. They were trained in the development, teaching and application of the Old Testament law. You can find the prophecy of verse 6 in Micah 5:2.

The wise men, after seeing the child Jesus, and being warned in a dream, returned to the east a different way. The message of the story of the wise men is important. Christ is a challenge to other religious beliefs, especially in the east and Far East, even today. It is important that we recognize Jesus' birth was probably known in all nations. He came not just as the King of the Jews, but He came to be the redeemer of all lost humanity. There was a feeling of expectancy in the land. The Jews were expecting a king to lead them out of their oppression. They were expecting a king to overthrow the Romans. They thought they would rule the world.

While we are coming to the celebration of Jesus' birth we know the king has come. He will come again and when He comes again He will rule the world. We need to look forward expectantly for Jesus to return. We don't know when that will be so we have to be ready for Him when He does come. We need to make sure we are where He expects us to be when He comes. We can't be like the six virgins who did not have enough oil to keep their lamps lit. We have to have our oil, our faith, trimmed and ready to welcome Him on His arrival. We need to know we are in the right place with Him. We have to stand firm and not waver in our waiting.

Have a good day and God bless!

Advent Week 2 day 5

Good morning:

As you light the Prophecy and Hope Candles today ponder these things; our reading is Luke 1:5-38. The story of Zechariah and Elisabeth, how in their old age God used them to be the parents of John the Baptist, the forerunner to Jesus' ministry; how Zechariah laughed when the angel told him and why he lost his voice.

There are several accounts in scripture relating to the coming of our Lord and Savior. There were many prophecies in the Old Testament regarding His coming. The people didn't understand who He was and what He was coming to do. They continued to live the way they desired causing the nation of Israel to be in bondage, held against their will, in Egypt and Babylonia. During the time of the birth of Christ they were bring oppressed by the Roman Government, They were anticipating the coming of the Messiah, but they were looking for someone who would come and overthrow the current government and remove their oppression. They weren't looking for a baby who would, later in life, come to give them eternal life.

The people involved in the event are very special people and what their part was gets put on the back burner, so to speak. Many don't take the Scripture of Zechariah and Elisabeth as part of the Christmas story, but without them part of God's plan would not have been complete.

We need to look to Luke 1:26-38 to the angel visiting Mary; she was a young girl, perhaps as old as 14, who had an angel appear to her one day and inform her that God had chosen her to be the mother of His son. How many of us would have been as gracious as Mary was. First off, she had never been with a man, secondly she was to marry a man named Joseph, third she would be an outcast in her family and village for having a baby before she had a husband.

Kay Ashwell

In our culture today this wouldn't even bother a lot of people. Back then it was a very big thing. But Mary didn't even once say no. She asked how it could be since she was a virgin, but when told she said;

> Luke1:38, "I am the Lord's servant," Mary answered, "may it be to me as you have said."

She loved the Lord and was willing to serve Him regardless of what that would mean to her as an individual. Remember her age was around 14; are you as willing to serve our Lord today as readily as she was in her day?

We move on to Joseph, a young man probably only a few years older than Mary, he was to take her as his wife, but finds out she is carrying a child. He was a righteous man and didn't want her to through public disgrace he had in mind to divorce her. Probably knowing what the scuttlebutt around town would be. Matthew 1:19-25

> Matthew 1:20-21; "But after he had considered this, an angel of the Lord appeared to him in a dream and said, Joseph, son of David, do not be afraid to take Mary home as your wife, because what is conceived in her is from the Holy Spirit. She will give birth to a son, and you are to give him the name Jesus, because he will save his people from their sins."

> Matthew 1:24-25, "When Joseph woke up, he did what the angel of the Lord had commanded him and took Mary home as his wife. But he had no union with her until she gave birth to a son. And he gave him the name Jesus."

Two individuals who, without question, did as God had directed them to do. This is *love*, this is *devotion*, this is *trust*, and this is *faith*. Do we have the same love, devotion, trust and faith in our God as these two young people had? I think I am safe to say *no*, many of us don't because if we did, this world would not be in the shape it is in today.

Without the faith and trust in God these two individuals had, we wouldn't have a Christmas story. Without our Lord being willing to leave heaven and come into this corrupt world we wouldn't be able to have eternal life with Him in paradise.

What about the most important person in the Christmas story, Jesus. Do you think He didn't know what was going on? Yes, He was a baby, but He was also God. He could have said no at any time, I'm going back to heaven. He didn't, He stayed and took all the abuse a human would endure and more, why? Because He loved us, His creation, enough to go through it all so we would have an opportunity to be with Him in eternity.

We need to stop thinking about what we want and start working toward what God wants for us and for the rest of the human race. It is time we start putting God first in our lives. When we do that He is going to help us get out of the messes we have created by doing things our own way and we can start doing the things He asks us to do. He has to become first in our lives each day. He is just waiting for you to say, here I am Lord, use me as you see fit. Then and only then will we know the peace and joy that He can give us. It's free for the asking, why not ask for it? What are you waiting for?

Have a great day and God bless!

Advent Week 2 Day 6

Good morning:

Today's story is found in Matthew 2:13-23 which I would like you to read. We learned a couple days ago that the wise men went to the palace in search of the Messiah and were told He was to be born in Bethlehem so they went to find Him. They were told in a dream, to not go back to the palace so they went home by a different route. This was the first event showing God's protection of His Son.

Today's passage speaks of further protection of God. Joseph is warned to take the child and his mother and go into Egypt. As believers in Christ we receive this same protection from God. He is always trying to warn us of dangers in our lives. The wise men and Joseph listened to these warnings why is it we are unable to recognize a warning when we are given one?

The events on 9/11 are full of stories of people not getting to the towers before the horror happened. The stories of people being stuck in traffic; missing the bus, of being held up for one reason or other are all stories of God's protection.

God is seeing what is happening, but is He hearing from His people regarding them? Are we making enough noise, saying enough prayers, or are we like the church in Laodicea, Revelation 3:14-22; are we neither hot nor cold? It's like riding a fence, we are either for or against Him, and we can't be both.

The church needs to become *hot* for Christ. We can't continue to just sit back in our easy chairs and say, 'Oh it will be all right.' It won't be alright because Satan doesn't want it to be alright. He is out to become bigger than God. That's why he was kicked out of heaven; he thought he should become God. That is his goal. Are we going to sit around and do nothing or are we going to stand up and be counted? There are more professing Christians in American than there are non believers. Why are we letting this happen? I can tell you why, because we are lazy, we don't want people to not like us so we just go along and don't stand up for what we believe.

There is a song called 'Where's the line to see Jesus?' Lyrics and music by Becky Kelly;

Take time to listen to it. It is a simple song, but it is one we all need to think about. We have long lines in most every store for people to see Santa, but we never see a line to see Jesus.

Too many just play the game of being for Him, but when the test really comes they can't stand their ground, they give into what is easiest to do. Walking with Christ is not an easy road, it is hard and full of holes and pitfalls, but when we are strong in Him we can come through them because our Lord and Savior is there with us, walking every mile with us.

As we come to the center of Advent look at yourself and your family, are you taking a stand for Jesus or are you just playing the part and not giving it your all? Think about what you can do to make a difference to someone else. What can you do to show others that you are Christ's and nothing will turn you from that? Maybe we should all make a *'line for Jesus'* in our hearts, our homes, our community and then to the world.

I pray each person comes closer to God today and each day; becoming stronger in your faith, and being able to trust Him enough to give yourself to Him, so He can lead your footsteps. So you can become a link for someone else to find Him. Be strong in your faith.

Have a great day and God bless!

Advent Week 2 Day 7

Good morning:

Today is the end of week two of Advent. Our scripture today Romans 12:9-21, it is not about the birth of Christ; it is about, *love, hope,* and *joy.* These attributes represent the whole meaning behind Christmas. This week we have been lighting the Hope Candle.

> Romans 12:12 "Be joyful in hope, patient in affliction, faithful in prayer."

These three things are very important when we are going through the dark valleys of our lives. To know that Christ is with us gives us the joy of hope, things will get better with His help. We don't usually think of joy and hope as going together, but they do. They go better together than the proverbial horse and carriage. *Joy is found in hope, and hope comes forth out of the joy in our hearts; the joy of knowing and serving our Lord.*

This passage in verse 9 also says love must be sincere. This reminds me to my favorite Scripture on love,1 Corinthians 13:1-13.

> Romans 12: 10 "be devoted to one another in brotherly love," In I Corinthians 13: 4-8a it tells us what love is and what love is not. "Love is patient, love is kind, it does not envy, it does not boast, it is not proud. It is not rude, it is not self-seeking, it is not easily angered, it keeps no record of wrongs. Love does not delight in evil but rejoices with the truth. It always protects, always trusts, always hopes, and always perseveres. Love never fails."

This kind of love is what each of us must strive for. Read it again, slowly, thinking about how you react to things, then decide how you have to respond differently in situations that arise each day. I think in today's world it is hard to be able to love without remembering what Christ has done for us.

Our prayer should be every day, *Lord let me love the way you love.* When we are truly seeking to love that way we will notice, before long, that it is easier to be positive and that we have given up the negative side of things. Then comes the *joy* in our heart and with that the *hope* of better things to come.

This Christmas season I encourage you to experience the joy of the celebration of the birth of the Savior. Focus your hope on the things above. God has a wonderful plan for His children. I challenge you, feast on the *bread of life,* Jesus. Respond with *joy* from the depths of your soul, and look forward with great *hope* knowing that the God who sent His Son for you is working faithfully in your life. Take the *hope* wherever you go, this world needs it.

Have a great day and God bless!

Advent Week 3 Day 1

Good morning:

As we start week three remember what the two prior candles mean; the first was the Prophecy Candle, which reminds us of the prophets who told of Jesus' birth; the second, the Bethlehem Candle which reminds us of the *hope* we have in Jesus, and today the third and pink one is the Shepherds Candle which reminds us of the *joy* and *celebration* of His birth. The candles remind us each day that Jesus is the *Light of the World.* The shepherds got to share in the initial announcement of the birth of Jesus.

Luke 2:8-20 tells how the shepherd's world was lit up by angels on the night of His birth. You need to read this Scripture. The joy they must have felt as they were the first to see Him.

His coming in a manger, with the angel's announcement of His birth to lowly shepherds in the field, reminds us of the rough simplicity of His birth. He wasn't sent to just a few; He was sent to be the savior of everyone. He died on the cross to take the sins of the world out of the way so man could find their way to Him and be free from them. He came in a manger, as a common person, to show God's love for everyone.

In our house, since 1998, we read a part of Jotham's Journey, an advent book. We read it when we light our candles each night. It's a storybook for Advent written by Arnold Yreeide. This is a story of a young Jewish boy who is searching for his family. It tells of his adventures, his trials, his searching his own heart, and along the journey he learns of the baby Jesus. In the end he finds who he is, the baby Jesus, and his family. There are many such books available. It makes Advent more meaningful when each night you share together this search for life. Even a single person can gain a closer walk with Jesus during Advent by doing this. Children love to have a story read to them before bedtime.

I would like to suggest you get a book for next year, most are on sale in Christian book stores. In that way when it is the fourth Sunday before Christmas and you get your wreath and candles ready you will have a special time together each evening.

I am glad the story of the shepherds is here to remind me that Jesus is my Shepherd. He came in a humble way to remind me that He knows who I am. In Hebrews we are told that Jesus knows who we are because He was, and still is, one of us. This reminds me of a European monarch, I can't remember his name at the moment, who would dress as a peasant and walk among the people. His court was concerned for his safety and asked him not to put himself in harm's way. He replied, 1 can't rule unless I know how they live. Jesus does know how we feel; He has been there before us.

In Luke 15:3-7 Jesus tells a parable of the lost sheep, there is also a song called The Ninety and Nine. Read this passage and remember Jesus is our Shepherd, and just as a real shepherd has to reach out with his staff and bring back into the flock stray sheep; He has to reach out and bring us back when we stray. There are many, many out there in this world who don't know Him, there are many out there who have strayed and haven't found their way back. We need to be their shepherd, reaching out to them where they are, gently bringing them back into the family. Jesus came to be a light to the world, He died to take the sins away and to offer eternal life to His people. He left us with a job, to be the shepherds, to these people; to be the light of His *love, hope,* and *joy* in this world.

Where are you, are you one who has strayed and haven't come back? Just reach out to Him, He will bring you back. Are you one who knows the Shepherd but haven't gone in search of a lost soul? The time is now to be that light that shepherd to someone else. People don't need us being better than them, they don't need us telling them what they have done wrong, they need us to be the shepherd that reaches out and gently brings them back into the family. The world needs to see Hi *love,* His *hope,* and His *joy.*

Have a great day and God bless!

Kay Ashwell

Advent Week 3 Day 2

Good morning:

Today as you light the three candles, Prophecy, Bethlehem, and Shepherd; I want you to think deeper about a shepherd. David, the author of the Psalms, knew about shepherds: he was one before he became a king. When you read Psalm 23 look at what he is really saying. God sent the greatest Shepherd to the world on Christmas.

Psalm 23:1a, "The Lord is my Shepherd."

This opening statement of the Psalm immediately implies a profound, practical relationship between a human being and his maker. It links man to divine destiny; it means a man becomes part of God. To think that I, a mere mortal, have a connection to God, gives me confidence to move on in life. Sheep cannot survive without a shepherd. They need constant care, just like we humans need the care of our heavenly Father. A good shepherd takes his sheep to the best pasture for food, he leads them to the clean water; he makes sure they are in a safe place to rest, he cares for their wounds. Jesus is our good Shepherd.

Psalm 23:1b, "I shall not be in want."

This means he will provide for our needs. Some think that after they are following the good shepherd they won't have any more problems. *That just is not true*, we have to understand we still live in a sinful world and our lives will have trials and hard times.. We have the promise of the good Shepherd to be with us through it all when those times come. He is there to show us the path we need to take, we only have to be smart enough to let Him show us which one it is and follow it.

Psalm23:2a, "He makes me lie down in green pastures,"

Sheep won't lie down and rest unless four things are present: There has to be no friction within the flock; there needs to be calmness and peace. They stay on their feet when flies and parasites are present in the flock and they will not lie down, when they stay on their feet it helps get rid of the parasites. They are timid creatures so if they fear they are not in a safe place they will not lie down. They will not lie down if the pasture they are in is not supplying their need for good nourishment.

So a flock that is restless, discontented, always agitated and disturbed never does well. How like sheep is the human race!! But as a Christian we are aware that our Shepherd is nearby, His presence in our lives can dispel the fear, the panic, and the terror of the unknown.

> 2 Timothy 1:7, "For God has not given us the spirit of fear; but of power, and of love, and of a sound, disciplined mind."

A sound mind is one at ease, at peace, not perturbed, harassed, or obsessed with fear and worry over the future.

> Psalm 23:2b, "he leads me beside quiet waters."

Sheep won't drink from a stream that is running fast, they fear being caught up in it and drowning. They will only drink in calm water. We, like them, don't do well when our life is running too fast, if we live in the fast lane too long we feel like our life is out of control, there is no balance in it. But when we have Christ we can drink from the cup of calm reassurance that He is not going to let us drown.

> Psalm 23:3, "He restores my soul."

To a shepherd this statement rings true because there are some sheep who for one reason or another get on their back and they can't get up and will eventually die without the shepherds help, it's called a 'cast down' sheep. There are times in our lives when we feel cast down, rejected, dejected, frustrated, tempted, bitter and feeling hopeless with no strength to go on. But when we call on our Lord to help us He is there to lift us up, to restore us to the proper place, to give us the calmness in our spirit. He gives us the desire to keep going, to keep trying and as long as we drink from the calm cup He offers us we will overcome these feelings of helplessness.

I could go on with each line of this Psalm but that would take too much time. But as you think on the light from the Shepherds Candle remember our good Shepherd was given to us on Christmas as a gift. He wants to be the light in our world, He wants to give to us the gifts that God intends for us to have. We need only reach out to Him and He will be there to restore us, to give us the things this world cannot give; the *love, hope, joy* and *peace* that only comes from knowing and following Him. Give your hurts, your disappointments, your broken hearts, your disobedience to Him this Christmas and receive the love and peace, hope and joy that a life lived in Him will give you.

Have a great day and God bless!

Advent Week 3 Day 3

Good morning:

Light your three candles and as you do focus your minds on the shepherds who were in the fields that night, as recounted in Luke 2:8-20.

We are going to look at these verses today and not just read them. Jesus is our Shepherd and He brought the light into a dark world. Christians are the light in the darkness of someone else's life.

A shepherd is someone who has to keep a close eye on his sheep because they stray and can get mixed in with another flock very easily. Verse 8 says, there were shepherds, keeping watch at night. There were many flocks of sheep on the hills and in the valleys on that day. They had to keep their flocks far enough away from one another to prevent the mixing with other flocks. So close your eyes and imagine for a minute looking at a hillside with a dozen different little fires and a dozen different groups of sheep.

> Luke 2: 9-12,"An angel of the Lord appeared to them. Do not be afraid, I bring you good news of great joy that will be for all the people. Today in the town of David a savior has been born to you; he is Christ the Lord. This will a sign to you; you will find a baby wrapped in clothe and lying in a manger."

Sheep are easily frightened, and tend to run about wildly when frightened. You would think this bright light and voices from nowhere would have frightened the sheep and the shepherds would have been busy keeping their flocks together. But that's not what it says, so I think God kept the animals quiet and calm so the shepherds could hear the message being given them.

They must have come together at some point in order for the shepherds, to talk together. I don't know how you would feel in this experience, but as I

Kay Ashwell

think about it, I would probably be a little frightened, yet at the same time a little awestruck; my heart would probably have been beating rather fast.

Think about what this would have looked like to them; a beautiful light in the dark night, and many voices singing from this light.

> Luke 2:13-14, "Suddenly a great company of heavenly host appeared with the angel, praising God and saying, Glory to God in the highest, and on earth peace to men on whom His favor rests."

Look at the rest of these verses because this is what I want to focus on today. These shepherds did five things after seeing and hearing the angel; six things over and above leaving their flocks; which apparently did not get frightened and were still lying quietly.

- They were able to see and hear this message from the Lord and still remain calm enough to come together from all over the hill.
- They seemed to know who sent the angel. The lowliest ones of their culture were expecting the Messiah. They apparently knew and understood the teachings of the time. They were not surprised that God had come through on His promises. I think today we miss little miracles that happen because we are not looking for them, we are not expecting them. Why aren't we? They have been promised to us.
- They responded right away. They didn't wait until morning; they didn't wait to find out if it was true. They went immediately to find the miracle.

Luke 2: 15, "When the angel had left them and gone into heaven, the shepherds said to one another, let us go to Bethlehem and see this thing that has happened, which our Lord has told us about."

How often do we go immediately and do something we know the Lord has told us to do? Most of us wait until it is convenient for us to do what has been asked. How often do we go pick up the phone and call someone who is on our minds, probably put there by God? How often has someone needed something and we ignore the need and go on about our day until our duties are done and then see what they need? The shepherds didn't wait, they went and found the baby.

- They did not doubt what they had been told. It must have seemed strange to them, a baby as a savior, born in a stable, and the place where animals sleep. Today people would just laugh and say that's impossible, no one goes to a stable to have a baby. We question everything, we have to have the answers to all questions before we step out and grasp hold of it, and even then we have doubts and more questions. We are not expecting a miracle so when it comes we can't even recognize it.
- In verse 17, after they saw the infant, they told everyone about Him and what had happened. They didn't keep this miracle to themselves; they shared it with everyone they saw. I imagine there were many who didn't believe them, after all why would the Savior be born in a stable and why would angels come to the shepherds and tell them. Again, the people were not expecting a miracle, they weren't able to recognize one when it was right in front of them.

The truth is God chose these circumstances to let the common people, the lowliest people, know that He was there for them, not just for the rich and famous, but for the common man. The ones who have to labor, the ones who are hurting, the ones who don't think they are good enough, the ones who are lonely. God sent Jesus into the world to give the people hope for a better life, hope for the future.

The shepherd's had a simple faith and received a rich reward, the reward of eternal life with the Savior. We can have that same simple faith; we just have to believe what God says and trust God to keep His promise. If you give your heart and mind and soul to Him, you will receive that hope that love, that joy and that peace which He promises to those who believe in Him.

Luke 2: 20, "The shepherds returned, glorifying and praising God for all the things they had heard and seen; which were just as they had been told."

- They were glorifying and praising God.

That's easy when things are going the way we want them to go. What happens when our world is turned upside down, when we don't think we can carry on? He is still there waiting for us to call out to Him, waiting to give us those promises. We simply need to ask, His promises are there, we can't find them if we don't ask Him for them. We have to go to Him just as the shepherds had to go to find Him that first Christmas night.

Don't wait, find Him now, and ask Him to help you through your troubles and trials. You won't be disappointed. It's a promise from God, all who seek Him will find Him and they will be healed.

Have a great day and God bless!

Advent Week 3 Day 4

Good Morning:

As I have prepared for my Sunday school class this week I can't fail to recognize all the unsaid things from the Christmas story. Like Mary, just being willing to be a servant to God and graciously accepting the call of God on her life. Without question she offered herself to Him.

> Luke 1:38, "I am the Lord's servant, Mary answered, may it be to me as you have said."

That is pure love. Love for God, love that has no boundaries.

Joseph was willing to obey what God had called him to do. Not being concerned about what the future would bring, just obeying God's call on his life.

> Matthew 1: 24; "When Joseph woke up, he did what the angel of the Lord had commanded him and took Mary home as his wife".

Look at the shepherds who left their flocks and went and found the baby.

> Luke 2:16; "So they hurried off and found Mary and Joseph, and the baby, who was lying in a manger".

They must have loved God, because they seemed to believe the angel. They had to go find God's son and worship Him without fear or hesitation. We should all have the same obedience to God as all these people did.

> Luke 2:19, "But Mary treasured up all these things and pondered them in her heart."

The word pondered means, to think seriously about something. Even though Mary knew that her son was the Son of God, she did not know what that was going to mean in His life. She was treasuring everything and I believe in this verse she was seriously thinking about what life would look like for Jesus and for them. After all God had just announced to the world that His Son had been born.

It could be a little disconcerting to have the world know that your son was the Son of God. How would you be feeling? Would you be feeling worthy of such an honor? Mary was willing to walk this walk with God but I'm sure she was wondering what it would look like. I'm sure she was thinking about what would happen in the future. Thoughts like, how long will I have Him, when will God call Him, will He be a normal boy; the same thoughts that any mother has at the birth of a son, only this was no ordinary son, this was the Son of God.

What about Joseph, he had also been called to care for this child, this Son of God. We know little about Joseph, but I think he too was wondering what all this would mean to them. I also think he was humbled by the awesome responsibility of being a part of this most amazing birth. His obedience to God is worthy to record. He obeyed and kept the child safe by going to Egypt for safety when told to go by the angel.

> Matthew 2: 13; "When they had gone (the magi) an angel of the Lord appeared to Joseph in a dream. Get up, he said, take the child and his mother and escape to Egypt. Stay there until I tell you, for Herod is going to search for the child to kill him".

Think about that for a moment, he just up and left his land, his home, his livelihood and took the baby and his mother to a foreign land without question, without knowing what might lie ahead. That's total obedience to God. Are you as obedient to God's call?

The shepherds immediately went about praising and glorifying God. They didn't go back and wait for someone to come to them. They went to others and told them what had happened. Do we go about singing and praising God as readily? Are we going about praising Him to everyone we meet or do we wait to praise God until we know it is a safe time to do so, like in church where everyone expects it? Do we praise Him and glorify Him in our everyday experiences, to everyone we see. The shepherds did, and they weren't even liked by most people, they were often put down, made to feel inferior. But that didn't matter; they didn't care what others thought they just went about praising and glorifying God anyway. We should be as dedicated.

Yes, the stories of Christmas are a familiar one but are the lives of those who were a part of it as familiar? Are their acts of obedience to God as familiar? Do we notice how God protected them, how He took care of them? They were worthy to be the parents of our Savior. They were obedient to God in every area of life.

Time after time scripture tells us to thank, praise and worship God.

> Ephesians 5:20, "always giving thanks to God the Father
> for everything, in the name of our Lord Jesus Christ."

This Christmas let us be thanking Him not only for the birth of His Son, Jesus, but for the gift that was given, for the love which was sent to us. Let us be thankful and praise Him for the many blessings He has given us, praise Him for who He is, and worship Him in all we think, say, and do.

As you think about what to give family and friends, *think about what you can give to God.*

What is He worthy of in your life? Where is He in your life? What are you willing to give to Him, the one who has given you everything? Are you ready to give Him your life? Are you willing to give up the things of this world and live only for Him?

Ponder on these things, make a decision, and then be willing to act on that decision. Nothing in this life is easy, but I can assure you that when you have Him in control of your life things will be easier to deal with. Isn't it time to give yourself to Him and find that *joy*, that *hope*, that *love* that is Christmas?

Have a great day and God bless!

Advent Week 3 Day 5

Good morning:

Light your three candles. We have looked at Mary and Joseph and the shepherds, so today let's look at the wise men. These men had traveled a long way and wanted to find the place where the child was. It is estimated that their arrival was some time after the birth, we don't know exactly how long. He is called a child here and not a baby so some feel he was a toddler. Read Matthew 2:1-13, when you read it remember that Herod was a very selfish person who would kill anyone who even appeared to be a threat to his reign.

The wise men were from another land, probably Persia. They were undoubtedly astrologers who had studied the skies and knew that a new star meant something great was to happen. We know little about them, about their beliefs, but we do know they must have some knowledge of the scriptures.

> Matthew 2:2 "Where is the one who has been born king of the Jews?"

We don't know if they were believers or not but they left their land, their work to find the one spoken of in the scriptures. Their need to find the child kept them going.

They were sent to Bethlehem with the instructions to return to Herod and tell him where the child was.

> Matthew 2:12 "And having been warned in a dream not to go back to Herod, they returned to their country by another route".

Kay Ashwell

This tells us that they were following or believing in God in some way. At the very least they believed enough to listen and follow what was said by an angel in a dream.

In this passage we also see Joseph having a dream and taking Mary and Jesus into Egypt for safety.

> Matthew 2:13, "When they had gone, an angel of the Lord appeared to Joseph in a dream. Get up, he said, take the child and his mother and escape to Egypt. Stay there until I tell you, for Herod is going to search for the child to kill him.

Again Joseph doing exactly what God is telling him without question; just doing it. The whole story of the birth of Christ is an amazing one, not only because of who He is, but because of all those involved following exactly what God is asking of them, without question.

Psalm 100 is a Psalm of thanks, usually associated with our Thanksgiving holiday. But it is one each of us needs to hold in our hearts at all times. As we remember those who were apart of the birth of our Savior we need to sing praises and be thankful for their devotion to God, for if any one of them had not followed God's instructions we would not have Jesus in our lives; we would not have the promise of eternal life. The miracle of the birth of Christ is more than a baby being born, more than a nice story. It is about people chosen by God for a great purpose, who loved Him enough to do as He asked them to do. It is a story of pure love, love from God toward man and love of people toward God. Yes, we should all put Psalm 100 to memory.

> Psalm 100: 1-5, "Shout for joy to the Lord, all the earth, Worship the Lord with gladness; come before Him with joyful songs. Know that the Lord is God. It is He, who made us, and we are His; we are the people, the sheep of His pasture. Enter His gates with thanksgiving and His courts with praise; give thanks to Him and Praise His

name. For the Lord is good and His love endures forever; his faithfulness continues through all generations."

This Psalm is a call to Praise God, to shout for *joy*. In the middle of this fast pace of our lives, it is often hard to sense any joy at all. Look at those around you, the ones you see each day at your job; do they look like they have joy? We live in the wealthiest nation in the world, yet we run here and there trying to find that magic *thing* that will bring us happiness.

Oh, it will make us happy for a little while, then we realize we still don't feel that special something. That's because that special something is put there by God to draw us to Himself. When we finally realize we can only find that special thing by knowing our Lord; for it is He who made us and we are His. When we know Him as our Father then we will know the real *joy*, real *peace*, real *love* we have been searching for.

This year, in fact this day, decide whose you are, decide you want that joy, peace, and love that is just waiting for you to ask for it, just waiting for you to take hold of it. Now is the time to turn your live over to Him, to allow Him to guide and direct your path, to have His love fill you with joy.

Have a great day and God bless!

Advent Week 3 Day 6

Good morning:

As you light the candles today remember what they are and what they stand for; the first was the Prophecy Candle and told of all the times the people were told about the coming of the Messiah; the second was the Bethlehem Candle and told us about the history and why Bethlehem was the city of his birth; the third is the Shepherds Candle.

Today read Luke 2:21-40 and find another amazing part of the story.

Eight days after his birth Jesus is taken to the temple in Jerusalem. The law required that the parents of a first-born son dedicate him to God. In this passage we find three rituals performed:

First was the circumcision of the child. This ritual signified his identification with the people of God. During the time when Moses led the people out of Egypt, God gave to them the law and instructions on what they where to do. Each male had to be circumcised signifying they were His people.

Second was the redemption of the first-born. Every first-born male, both human and animal was sacred to God. A sum of five shekels was given to the priests to redeem or buy back their first-born son.

Third was purification. This was to purify the mother for uncleanness in childbirth. Mary and Joseph could only afford the sacrifice of the poor, "a pair of doves and 2 young pigeons".

All three ceremonies showed that a child was a gift from God.

There is a lot more in these verses though. We have Simeon, a righteous and devout man. This passage tells me he was a man who loved and believed in God and His promises to the people of Israel. He had obviously heard from God and was looking expectantly for the Messiah.

Luke 2: 25-32, "Now there was a man in Jerusalem, who was righteous and devout. He was waiting for the consolation of Israel, and the Holy Spirit was upon him.. It had been revealed to him by the Holy Spirit that he would not die before he had seen the Lord's Christ. Moved by the Spirit he went into the temple courts. When the parents brought in the child Jesus to do for him what the custom of the Law required, Simeon took him in his arms and praised God, saying; Sovereign Lord, as you have promised, you now dismiss your servant in peace. For my eyes have seen your salvation; which you have prepared in the sight of all people, a light for revelation to the Gentiles and for glory to your people Israel."

Simeon had been waiting patiently, expectantly for the Messiah. It also tells us that here again God blessed those who were devout believers by revealing to them what was to come. His Spirit was with them.

This story of Christmas is God's promise to the nation of Israel that He was fulfilling the promises and the prophecy of the Old Testament. This was to be a new beginning for them and for the Gentiles. A new beginning in the form of a baby who would grow to be like God in every way, yet who was born on earth so He could show the world how to walk with God, by experiencing everything that man goes through. Jesus is more than a prophet, a good man, as many believe; in truth He is the Messiah; the savior of the World.

This Christmas can be a new beginning for you too. This baby born In Bethlehem came to show each of us, and the world that by believing in Him and believing in the *hope, joy* and *love* that it represents. We too can have the *peace* which is promised. It's there for us to take if we ask Him to come to us. We have only to ask, He won't just come on His own, and He won't force Himself on us. He knocks at the door of our hearts; we have to open that door. We have to take the step of believing in Him and in knowing we can't do things on our own any longer. We need Him to show us how. Then He comes to us and offers us that Peace, that Hope, that Joy and that Love we have been searching for. Today can be that day for you.

Have a great day and God bless!

Advent Week 3 Day 7

Good morning:

Today is the end of the third week of Advent which means Christmas is only a few days away. Tomorrow we will light all the colored candles. For today as you light the Prophecy, the Bethlehem, and the Shepherd Candles read Luke 2: 9-40. Think about Mary and Joseph, these simple verses tell us the depth of character they had.

As we have learned in past days, they were willing and ready to allow God to use them for this most important event in history. They were willing to help God fulfill His promise to His people. Mary was willing to endure gossip, rejection, and the threat of death. Joseph was willing to suffer ridicule, embarrassment, and shame. They traveled to Bethlehem and endured the birth, in a stable, before they were married. They could have been removed from the families, or sent away from the town, but they followed all the prescribed procedures of their religion and God was with them.

Throughout all of this did you once hear *why me, God,* or *this isn't fair,* or *can you make this a little easier?* The answer is a resounding no. All we have seen is two young people loving and respecting their God. We see faithful obedience. No wonder God chose them to be the earthly parents of our Lord and Savior. He knew He could depend on them.

When I think of people today who claim to be Christians, yet who go about with a negative attitude, I wonder where their faith lies. It can't be in my Savior, because He doesn't show us negative things. He gives us warmth from the sun, light in the darkness from the moon, rains so we have water. He provides us with food in abundance, loves us, forgives us, gives us air to breathe, and provides all kinds of beauty for us to see. Yet, the world sees with selfish eyes and cannot see that God has provided all we need, and gives us more besides.

Kay Ashwell

Where do you stand? Are you willing to give God your all; are you willing to be faithful and obedient regardless of the consequences? The story of Jesus birth and the people involved in it should challenge us to be more obedient and faithful in our service to Him. He sent His son to give His all for each of us. Are we willing to give our all to Him in return?

As Christmas comes ever closer, and as we celebrate the birth of Jesus, we need to look at where we are with Him, where we have been with Him this past year. Have we been faithful to Him, have we allowed Him to guide us every day, have we obeyed His calling in our lives?

We need to be honest with ourselves and with God. We need to decide to follow Him more closely in the coming year. Our challenge and our prayer should be, help me be more obedient, more faithful, more loving in all I say and do. Help me draw closer to you each day. The decision is ours. Are we willing to make it?

Have a great day and God bless!

Advent Week 4 Day1

Good morning:

Today is the last Sunday before Christmas and we light all four colored candles. The first one is the Prophecy Candle, the second the Bethlehem Candle, the third the Shepherd Candle and today we light the last purple candle the Angel Candle. This candle reminds us that the angels were messengers proclaiming Christ's birth to the shepherds. A familiar song at Christmas is 'Hark! The Herald Angels Sing,' proclaiming God's love. Listen to the words of this song, it tells us the Reason for the Season.

Hark! The Herald Angels Sing
"Glory to the newborn King!
Peace on earth, and mercy mild
God and sinners reconciled"
Joyful, all ye nations rise,
Join the triumph of the skies,
With th'angelic host proclaim;
"Christ is born in Bethlehem,"
Hark! The herald angels sing,
"Glory to the newborn King!"

Christ, by highest heav'n adored
Christ, the everlasting Lord!
Late in time behold Him come,
Offspring of a virgin's womb,
Veiled in flesh the Godhead see,
Hail the incarnate Deity,
Pleased as man with men to dwell,
Jesus, our Immanuel
Hark! The herald angels sing,
"Glory to the newborn King!"

Kay Ashwell

Hail, the heav'n born Prince of Peace!
Hail the Son of Righteousness!
Light and life to all He brings,
Ris'n with healing in His wings,
Mild he lays His glory by,
Born that man no more may die.
Born to raise the sons of earth,
Born to give them second birth.
Hark! the herald angels sing,
"Glory to the newborn King!"

Gabriel, the head angel, played a large part in the story of Christmas. He came to tell a virgin peasant girl she was to be the mother of the Son of God; the mother of the long-awaited Messiah. He instructed Joseph in a dream.The angels told the shepherds the good news after the birth. They gave the news to the poorest, least liked of all men. The angels stood watch over the place where Jesus lay.

Mary's *yes* to God, even though she knew that it would be scandalous, should be an encouragement for us to say *yes* to God when He enters our world and turns it upside down. But His plan is always best. Mary found that out.

Everyone is searching for something, each search for it in their own way, but until they come to know Jesus the search is in vain. Why, because what everyone is looking for is to know someone loves them. Jesus is that person. He loves us regardless of what we do. No, He is not always happy with us, but He always loves us. That is the reason God sent Him to us. To show us love, pure love, that comes only from God. Once we know that love we will no longer be searching for something we can't find.

Our lives will be complete. I know, for when I found His love I was content; there was peace in my soul. Yes, our search ends when we find Jesus, God's gift to man, love! Won't you come to Him this Christmas and know the peace I know. It's easy; just ask Him into your life and ask Him to forgive you for the sin in your life. He is waiting for you to come to Him.

Love came down at Christmas, take hold of that *love*!

Have a great day and God bless!

Kay Ashwell

Advent Week 4 Day 2

Good morning:

We are in the last few days before Christmas and the celebration of our Lord's birth. Today's scripture is Isaiah 40:10-11 and Isaiah 53:1-7. These verses give us a powerful message. Christmas is a day of hope.

Christmas is not just a day in December that comes and goes each year. It is not a day in December when we get lots of presents, some we want and some we don't. What Christmas is, however, is when our tears are wiped away, it is every time we have new hope in our dark world; it is every time a sinner is saved by God's grace. It is every time a heart is filled with the Holy Spirit, it is every time a blood-washed pilgrim enters into eternal life. It is the great hope of the gospel. This is what Jesus means to a dark and sinful world. This is why He was sent to us.

Our verses today tell of that hope;

> Isaiah 40: 10-11; "See, the Sovereign Lord comes with power and his arm rules for him. See, his reward is with him, and his recompense accompanies him. He tends his flock like a shepherd; he gathers the lambs in his arms and carries them close to his heart; he gently leads those that have young."

Yes our Lord comes with power, strength and gentleness. He comes to lead His people to reconciliation them to Himself.

Isaiah 53: 1-7 relates to us, how the world receives Him. Then tells us that by His death He has taken our sins to Himself and by His wounds we are healed.

Christmas should be to the world a time of new beginnings, but the world of today still does not recognize Him as the Savior of the world;

it still seeks after its own desires; the desires of men who want power, riches and control.

For those of us who call Christ our savior, or our brother, it is a time to renew our *hope*, our *joy*, our *peace*, and our *love*. It is a time to refresh our lives so others can see these things in us and know the Lord through us. Christ is the answer for this broken world, for this broken nation, for the broken hearted of our land. They don't see Him and they can't find Him without seeing Him in us. We are His light in this darkness.

He is depending on us to carry His love, His peace, His joy, and His hope to those who can't see. He is our good shepherd, are we a shepherd to the lost world? He taught us how, are we doing what He asks us to do? Sheep need a steady, caring hand, they need to be led to good food and water or else they eat and drink whatever is there and available to them. Are we the shepherds to those who need this gentle guiding hand or are we so wrapped up in our own world we neglect those who are crying in the desert?

Christmas is a time of renewal. A time when we remember why God sent Jesus to this world. Are we taking the time to renew our own spirits, to renew our own commitment to Him? Or are we letting the world pull us into the fast pace of gifts, wants, desires, parties and festivities to the point of not having time to stop and be blessed by the real reason we celebrate this day?

It's time to stop all the business and just renew our spirits with Him. The things of this world, the things of today don't mean a thing compared to what is waiting for us when He returns to take us to our real home. It's time to commit to Him the things that keep us from His love, from His hope, from His joy, and from His peace for us and for the world.

Have a great day and God bless!

Advent Week 4 day 3

Good morning:

Today light the four candles and let's read our scripture. Christ is identified as the Son of God and greater than the angels.

> Hebrews 1:1-4: "In the past God spoke to our forefathers through the prophets at many times and in various ways, but in these last days he has spoken to us by his Son, whom he appointed heir of all things, and through whom he made the universe. The Son is the radiance of God's glory and the exact representation of his being, sustaining all things by his powerful word. After he had provided purification for sins, he sat down at the right hand of the Majesty in heaven. So he became as much superior to the angels as the name he has inherited is superior to theirs."

This gives confirmation that God sent His son to earth to be able to give us a chance to be with Him in eternity.

Christmas is the celebration of this gift, the most wonderful gift in all of human history. God sent his Son, Jesus, who willingly came to redeem our world. The story of His birth is simple and beautiful. It is filled with love and peace and obedience.

Obedience of two young people who respected their God and followed and trusted what he asked of them. Their lives were changed by this selfless act of love. Our lives have been changed by His coming. Your life can be changed to reflect that love and peace. The world seems to stand still on Christmas. Things seem more peaceful, more respectful. This time of year, more than any other, people seem to share love and peace.

Some of you are going to say, that's not so. I agree up to the last few days our world has been very busy, very hectic, and very crude. But the last few days before Christmas people seem to settle down, they seem to be happier, they show more joy, they don't seem to be in such a hurry, they even stop and talk to you. That's because families are gathering together to share their memories, to share their love and joy with each other.

Many have family traditions they won't break, and some have discovered that celebrating the birth of Christ is one of them. Preparations are made for celebrating together. The weeks between Thanksgiving and Christmas are hectic and chaotic, but the last few days, seem more peaceful, more settled. There is more love and peace because families are coming together in peace and harmony.

The angels spoke of joy and peace; people have found that the joy and peace of Christmas is possible.. If you don't have family traditions of Christmas which focus on togetherness and slowing down, I suggest you start some. One of ours has always been to drive around on Christmas Eve and see all the wonderful lights, to feel the quietness in the air, to feel the joy of being together. We then go home, have a cup of hot chocolate, read the Christmas story again, and sit and talk about that first

Christmas night when our Lord was born. We are reminded of the love that was given on that night, of the joy in the hearts of those involved, and what that birth has meant to our world.

Yes, Christmas is only a few days away and you can already feel the love in the air. If you haven't felt that love and joy yet, perhaps it is because you have not shared your life with our Lord. Now is the perfect time to do that. He is the only one who can give you that peace and joy in your heart you are searching for. When you have given Him all your cares and worries, and accepted His love and forgiveness, you will be able to sing those carols because your heart will be overflowing. You will find Christmas to be very special.

My prayer for each of you is that you will slow down, take time to feel the love, take time to be with loved ones, or find someone who needs

Kay Ashwell

love and shower them with it. You take time to praise our Lord for the blessings He has given us. If you are alone, you can still feel the love and joy because Jesus is with you or wants to be with you.

Yes, love came down at Christmas; love needs to overflow from us to others. God's love needs to flow from us to those who need it.

Have a great day and God bless!

Advent Week 4 Day 4

Good morning:

December 23rd; it's two days until we celebrate our Savior's birth. Light your four colored candles and read Psalm 25. It is beautiful and shows the love and hope we have in our Savior.

> Psalm 25: 4-7, "Show me your way, O Lord, teach me your paths; guide me in your truth and teach me, for you are God my Savior, and my hope is in you all day long! Remember, O Lord, your great mercy and love, for they are from old. Remember not the sins of my youth and my rebellious ways; according to your love remember me for you are good, O Lord."

Read the whole Psalm, it will bless you.

Some still ask why He came in a stable, to poor parents. Why wasn't he born into royalty, after all, He is the king. For man to understand the purpose of His coming He had to come asking nothing for Himself, making no great noise, seeking no fame for Himself. We have seen enough in history and in the world today to know that being born into royalty, being well educated, being in power doesn't give us the answers we are all seeking.

He had to come for the downtrodden people, the common people who are hurting, for those who are down on luck, who are alone and afraid of the future and can't see there is a better way. He had to be strong enough to lift us from the grips of falsehood and the mire of make-believe; of prettied-up cosmetically covered up selfishness. He had to be real, genuine, with no pretense, and most of all He had to be able to identify with all mankind. He had to be humble; He had to come into this world in a meager estate so we would identify with Him. So we could know He understands how we feel. He had to have a profound love for each of us. We had to see that love through His life here on earth. *He came to bring us hope.*

Kay Ashwell

These are the reasons He came to earth as a baby, born in a stable, where He didn't have a place to lay His head, so people could know that He came to save them from this world. He came knowing what His life would be like here, but he was willing to leave heaven and come to earth so we would have a way to be in heaven with Him and have the hope we need to maintain in this life on earth.

I hope and pray you have taken time this Advent season to allow Him to come into your life, to strengthen you, to show you there is someone who loves you and cares for what you are going through.

I pray this Advent season has brought *joy, peace, hope* and *love* into your life. He can take your past and forgive you and forget your sins. He can make your future full of that hope, joy, love and peace you are searching for. Advent is almost over, don't miss it on your way to the tree and all the packages you have under it. If you don't have any under it, you really need to take hold of Him and find your future.

Advent in Latin means, coming or arrival. It is the season when Christ came to us; it is the season we prepare for His next arrival; the one where He will take us to be with Him. Advent should be grasped, held onto, not skipped over on the way to more self centeredness. It is a time to give yourself to Him all over again; if you never have given yourself to Him, it's not too late to get that hope, that joy, that peace and most of all the love that will never die, will never go away when you are His. Ask Him into your heart and soul and mind today.

I would suggest you each read Psalm 25 again. Be encouraged by what it says to each of us.

Come, sweet Jesus, come. The hope of Christmas is His returning to take us home to be with Him. Won't you join with us in that hope and ask Him into your life, all of it, not just part of it. The gift God gave is far greater than any you will receive under that Christmas tree. Don't miss Advent.

Have a great day and God bless!

Advent Week 4, Day 5

Good Morning:

In today's scripture Matthew 2:1-12 it tells of the wise men that followed the star to Bethlehem. We have touched on them in previous thoughts but verse 11 has some asking about the gifts they brought.

> Matthew 2:11, "On coming to the house, they saw the child with his mother Mary, and they bowed down and worshiped him. Then they opened their treasures and presented him with gifts of Gold, Frankincense and of Myrrh."

They certainly weren't the usual gifts brought to a king. Here is a short explanation of the gifts. Gold was the gift for kings; Frankincense was used by worshipers representing their ascending prayers of sinful actions to God; and. Myrrh was used in the embalming of the body. These three gifts are practical as well as symbolic; Gold representing Jesus as King; Frankincense shows Him as Priest; and the Myrrh representing Him as Savior. These are the three gifts given man on that first Christmas day, a king, a priest and a savior.

What does it mean to be Savior? The Savior we need must come from outside our world, because we know that everything in our world is tainted and spoiled. We are all tainted, sinful humans. We are not impressed with a Savior who comes speaking only the things we want to hear, nor would we be impressed with one who came only with grandeur. We have seen enough of them in history and behind all the pomp lurks a greedy, self-righteous man with only self-centeredness and greed as his focus.

Our Savior did not come in pomp. He came asking nothing for himself, making no great scene about Himself, seeking no fame. He must be strong in wisdom and love to be able to lift us out of our mire of sin,

Kay Ashwell

falsehood and unreality of the glossed up, prettied up, commercialism of Christmas that covers up selfishness in men.

He must be honest, genuine, and loyal. He must be able to identify with each person, personally. He must be humble so He can show us how to be humble, how to be thankful for what He has given us. That humble King came to us on Christmas. He has been called by many names over the years. Scripture says He is to be called Jesus, a grand name to the Jews. The name Jesus means "Yahweh," God is our salvation. He is also called Immanuel, meaning, God with us.

William Barclay in the Daily Study Bible, volume 1, page 14 says, "Jesus enables us to see what is and what man ought to be; Jesus opens the eyes of our minds so that we can see the truth of God for us; Jesus is the creating power which can release the souls of men from the death of sin."

The Gather's, a singing group, came out with a simple chorus a number of years ago, which when I hear it, it gives me peace and hope and love all wrapped in one. It's called, *Jesus*. There is something about that name, there is beauty in those words, there is wonder in the name Jesus, but when you say it you get such a peaceful feeling in your soul that nothing else can give you. The name is warm and inviting and that is what He is saying to us, I am inviting you to become a part of me, to live with me in eternity.

I hope, as you go through these last two days before His birth that you remember the gifts of the wise men, they represent who Jesus is. I pray that you know Him as I know Him, a loving, patient, understanding Father who loves me so much He was willing to die so I could join Him in heaven forever.

Look at the things of Christmas with new eyes today, the tree, the evergreen, which symbolizes a forever life, pointed, reaching to heaven. For those who may not know, the limbs of an evergreen tree are turned toward heaven, always pointing up.

As you wrap those last gifts, think about the gift that was wrapped and laid in the manger. The gift given by God to all of us.

If you know my Jesus, be at peace this day and each day, if you don't know my Jesus, now is the best time to ask Him into your life and become part of his family. You just have to ask.

Have a great day and God bless!

Kay Ashwell

Advent Week 4 Day 6

Good morning on this Christmas Eve:

Today or tonight whenever you light the four advent candles remember what they stand for; they are the Prophecy, the Bethlehem, the Shepherd, and the Angel Candles; then light the white, Christ Candle in the center, it symbolizes Christ's presence in our world. Now all the candles are burning. Christ comes, tonight, Christmas Eve. What a wonderful celebration of love. The world will be at peace today, at least in the worlds where Christ reigns; in your heart I pray. Tonight the light of the world comes. Let that light shine in your heart. Let that love fold you in His arms and take care of you.

> "O Come, O Come, Immanuel, and ransom captive Israel; that mourns in lonely exile here until the Son of God appear. O come, Thou Wisdom from on high, and orders all things far and nigh; to us the path of knowledge show, and cause us in your ways to go. Rejoice! Rejoice! Immanuel shall come to thee, O Israel."

Immanuel, what a beautiful name it is. He is God with us. He gives us wisdom, knowledge, understanding, love, joy, hope and peace. What a wonderful gift God has given us.

> Philippians 2:1-11 says, better than I, who He is, "If you have any encouragement from being united with Christ, if any comfort from His love, if any fellowship with the Spirit, if any tenderness and compassion, then make my joy complete by being like minded, having the same love, being one in spirit and purpose. Do nothing out of selfish ambition or vain conceit, but in humility consider others better than yourselves. Each of you should look not only to your own interests, but also to the interest of others. Your attitude should be the same

as that of Christ Jesus. Who, being the very nature God, did not consider equality with God something to be grasped but made himself nothing, taking the very nature of a servant, being made in human likeness, and being found in appearance as a man, He humbled Himself and became obedient to death, even death on a cross. Therefore God exalted Him to the highest place and gave Him the name that is above every name, that at the name of Jesus every knee should bow, in heaven and on earth and under the earth, and every tongue confess that Jesus Christ is Lord, to the glory of God the Father".

United in Christ, to be in Christ is to be saved. It is to be in an intimate personal relationship with Christ, the Savior. From this relationship comes all the benefits and the fruit of salvation, which includes encouragement and comfort from His love; the love which was given on Christmas. Mary wrapped our gift of love from God in clothe; we can wrap that same gift around someone who needs it today.

As you open your gifts this year remember the gifts God has given you and thank Him for each one.

If you haven't found that gift of love now is the perfect time to receive it. It is just waiting for you. Your life will take on a whole new turn when you reach out to Him and take hold of that gift of love.

If you haven't said that prayer, or asked God to help you, say it now! God I am a sinner and I do not deserve your love, but I can't live another day without you in my life. Please forgive me of my sinful past and walk with me from this time forward. Help me to be more like You, let me see others the way you want me to see them, with love, and teach me your ways so I may walk with you into eternity.

Have a wonderful Christmas Eve and God bless you and yours!

Christmas Day

Good morning and Merry Christmas:

Praise God! His gift of love and hope has been born.

As you open your gifts this morning, remember to unwrap the greatest gift of all, the gift of God's Son, unwrap this gift of love, hope, joy, and peace. Let it light your day and your life from today on into the New Year and into eternity.

There was an old woman in Luke 2:38 named Anna, she was close enough to God that she absolutely knew when the Christ child would be presented at the temple. She was expecting and looking forward to the day of the long-awaited Messiah. "At that very hour she began to give thanks to God and to speak of Him to all who were waiting for the redemption of Jerusalem."

> Titus 2:11-14; "For the grace of God that brings salvation has appeared to all men. It teaches us to say 'No' to ungodliness and worldly passions and to live self-controlled, upright and godly lives in this present age, while we wait for the blessed hope, the glorious appearing of our great God and Savior, Jesus Christ, who gave himself for us to redeem us from all wickedness and to purify for himself a people that are His very own, eager to do what is good."

This describes the effect grace should have on believers. It encourages rejection of un-godliness and encourages godly living. We should be looking forward to that day, the day when our Savior and King will come and call us home. We should be looking forward with great anticipation and joy to that day.

Today is a day of celebration; let it be the day of celebrating the 'Birthday of a King.' It is a day for singing praises to Him, to glorify His name and most of all remember to unwrap the gift of love He has given to each of us; a love which will last forever. He will never take it from us, He will never leave us, and He will always be there for us. We have to do the action of unwrapping it and allowing it to fill our hearts, our minds, and our souls.

Yes, today is the day of the Savior's arrival, look expectantly for His return. Look expectantly for the gifts He has planned for you this coming year, and above all, praise Him for all the things He has done, will do, and what He has planned for you in eternity. I pray each of you has come to know my Jesus this Advent season. He is the only thing we should be anticipating, nothing else in this world means anything if you haven't put Him first in your heart and life. He is the only thing that can get you from here to eternity.

On this Christmas day remember the birth of a baby that has come to set men free from sin and give them the hope of a better tomorrow. Don't stop with just remembering, carry it on; proclaim it with praise and a hallelujah for His return, it is closer than you think.

> Revelation 19:5-8 says, "Then a voice came from the throne, saying, 'Praise our God, all you his servants, you who fear him, both small and great! Then I heard what sounded like a great multitude, like the roar of rushing waters and like loud Peals of thunder, shouting: 'Hallelujah! For our Lord God Almighty reigns, Let us rejoice and be glad and give him glory! For the wedding of the Lamb has come and His bride has made herself ready; fine linen, bright and clean, was given her to wear." (Fine linen stands for the righteous acts of the saints.)

The Lamb is Jesus, the bride is His church, His people and the saints are those who have followed His ways and allowed Him to rule in their lives. His return is close, are you ready? Are you looking forward to that day? Have you invited Him into your life to live there and guide you and be first in your life? If you haven't you have not yet unwrapped the gift sent by God on that first Christmas Day.

Please, take time today to unwrap that precious gift and allow love, hope, joy and peace enter into you. Be wrapped in His love today and every day until the day comes when He calls us to our real home in eternity with Him.

Have a blessed day and God bless!

Challenges

Challenge to pray for nation

Good morning:

First, Happy 4th of July; the day we celebrate the formation of our country. The Declaration of Independence was signed on this day in 1776 by five men form the Continental Congress. It broke officially the ties to Great Britain. It states that man has the right to life, liberty and the pursuit of happiness. Of the original signers of the document were two future presidents, John Adams and Thomas Jefferson. In a remarkable coincidence both died on July 4, 1826, exactly 50 years after the signing. One other president died on July 4, James Monroe, although he was not a signer of the document, he was the fifth president. Calvin Coolidge, the thirteenth president, was born on July 4, 1872. An important date in history.

The national anthem, The Star Spangled Banner, was written by Francis Scott Key in 1814 during the war of 1812. He had watched the bombardment of Fort McHenry, in the Chesapeake Bay, by ships of the British Royal Navy all night. He wrote four verses, the first of which is the only one well known.

The last verse reads:
O thus be it ever when free men shall stand
Between their loved homes and the war's desolation!
Blest with victory and peace, may the heaven rescued land
Praise the Power that hath made and preserved us a nation!
Then conquer we must, when our cause it is just;
And this be our motto, "In God is our trust"!
And the Star Spangled Banner in triumph shall wave
O'er the land of the free and the home of the brave.

The motto, 'In God we Trust' was adopted from this forth verse of the poem written by Mr. Key. Today, many people are trying to remove God from our Country, a country founded on Godly principles.

Today, that verse should be sung along with the first verse. The two give a picture of what our country stands for. It was built on Godly principles by men who were wiser than we are today. They knew what could happen to a nation if God was not at the center of all the decisions made. Scripture relates what we are to do.

God is speaking to Solomon in:

> 2 Chronicles 7:13-14, "When I shut up the heavens so that there is no rain, or command locusts to devour the land, or send a plague among my people, if my people, who are called by my name, will humble themselves and pray and seek my face and turn from their wicked ways, then shall I hear from heaven and will forgive their sin and will heal their land."

Look around at our nation today, it is not what our founding fathers would approve of, it is certainly not what God expects from us. We have become a nation filled with immoral acts which have even moved into the churches. People, called by His name, have turned their back on Him. Churches have turned their back on Scripture, making it say what they want it to say. We have become a people who are surviving on a watered down Christianity. People take faith lightly, and believers' seem to think they can do only what is absolutely necessary, and then only if they feel like it. I'm sure Jesus is disappointed in so many *fair weather* followers.

Scripture warns those who change the words of the Bible to suit themselves:

> Revelation 22: 18-20 "I warn everyone who hears the words of the prophecy of this book. If anyone adds anything to them, God will add to him the plagues described in this book. And if anyone takes words away from this book of prophecy, God will take away from him his share in the tree of life and in the holy city, which are described in this book. He who testifies to

Kay Ashwell

these things says, Yes, I am coming soon. Amen, come,
Lord Jesus"

In other words nothing can save anyone who changes, adds to or deletes anything from what is written in Scripture.

Today it is a day to celebrate our Country, but it is also a day when God's people, those who trust in Him, who believe in Him and who truly follow His ways, need to be on their knees giving Him praise and honor for what He has given us. We need to be praying for our country, for the people to open their eyes and turn back to the God who has provided for and protected this nation. We need to be in prayer that it is not too late for our nation. This nation stands for the freedom every person in the world wants.

The words of Francis Scott Key in Verse four of the Star Spangled Banner are words we all need to heed, *Blest with victory and peace, may the heaven rescued land Praise the Power that hath made and preserved us a nation. Then Conquer we must, when our cause it is just, and this be our motto, In God is our Trust.* God's people need to be in prayer for God's wisdom to once again be in the center of our nation.

In an arena in Houston, the governor of Texas, Rick Perry, held a day of prayer and fasting for our nation in August of 2011. There were no concessions, no big stars to see or hear, just a day of prayer. The following are some excerpts from the governor's message.

"Our founding fathers understood that it was a very important part of the pursuit of happiness. Being able to own things that are your own is one of the things that make America unique. But I happen to think that it's in jeopardy. It's in jeopardy because of taxes; it's in jeopardy because of regulation; it's in jeopardy because of a legal system that's run amok. And I think it's time for us to just hand it over to God and say, God, You're going to have to fix this."

I think it's time for us to use our wisdom and our influence and really put it in God's hands. That's what I'm going to do, pray, and I hope you'll join me. Here's what I want to leave you with. I know from time to time people say there goes another person who thinks prayer is the answer to everything. That's ok with me, prayer changes things.

I love our country. It was created by God. Individuals who understood those biblical values and how powerful they could be and would be in the future created a powerful nation. And I suggest that for our country, our best days are ahead if we'll get on our knees and ask God to take over and give us wisdom. I may wear the Lord out every day in prayer; I pray for restoration of this country; I pray for our president every day; I pray that God turns buckets of wisdom out on his head, that God will open his eyes. We can change this country, but it requires our giving it to Him and letting Him guide us.

I believe all true Christians should be in prayer and fasting, joining with thousands of others from across the nation for God to once again take control of this nation.

Have a great day and God bless!

Challenge to stand firm

Good morning:

Life is full of challenges, full of sorrows, and full of pain. For some that is all they see: pain and suffering from this life. They don't know there are also joy, hope, love, and forgiveness. They only know hurt. You may think those things are only in third world nations where there is nothing good going on. But, it is also very real to many, many people in the U.S. They don't know anything but suffering and pain. Some are born into homes where there is never enough to eat, or a home where they are beat for saying anything. Some are born to parents who only see their own hurt and use drugs to survive. Some are abused sexually to amuse others and to fulfill a perverted need. Some are raised to believe they are not needed or wanted by anyone; they just have to do what they are told before they can get any food. Some never have a chance to grow up, because no one cared enough to step in and change their life. Some young girls are even sold to be slaves to some rich person somewhere in the world. They are shipped out like cattle. Worst of all are those babies who never see life because they were aborted before they were even born by people who didn't want them.

Not a pretty picture is it. But that is going on right here in our own nation. Why? People don't want to get involved with their neighbors. They don't want to be bothered with the negative side of life. Just keep me happy, just give me what I want, it doesn't matter if someone else is suffering as long as I'm not and I have what I want.

God doesn't want His children to suffer at the hands of someone else. He expects those who claim to be Christian's to fight for, to care for, to be involved with those who are hurting. I don't care where you live in this country; someone is hurting; someone is in need of a friend. Someone is in need of a friendly smile, a kind word. Many are in need of Jesus. What are you doing to help? We need to each look at our daily walk, are we walking in Jesus' shoes and being Jesus to those around us? Or are we just doing what we have to do, what we want to do? Are we serving the kingdom or just ourselves?

What good are we if we only believe and do nothing to help? What good do we do when we only go to church on Sunday and perhaps Wednesday evening and sit in a pew and leave and do nothing for Him the rest of the week? Do you think God is happy with that? Do you think you are going to be called into eternity? That all you have to do is be in church when the doors are open! I have news for you, it is not enough, if you are truly one of His children you have been called to serve, to be a servant to others.

Christ was a servant. Being a servant is not waiting on someone hand and foot. Many people think to be a servant you are the lowest of humans. But that is not true. Slaves are bought and paid for to serve their masters every desire. A servant is one who sees a need and takes care of it. Jesus taught us in John 13 that we need to be humble, to be willing to do menial tasks for someone else's benefit. He washed His disciple's feet to impress upon them that He was not too good to serve their need. He set the example of selfless service. Yet He did it out of love, not out or duty.

He told Peter in John 13: 8 "unless I wash you, you will have no part with me".

There is another meaning to this verse, which I will address at a later time. But for today it symbolizes the need for us to be humble Christians and be willing, with the right heart, a heart of love for Jesus, to serve the needs of others.

It doesn't mean we get down and crawl in the dust to do what they want; it means we are to humbly be willing to provide what they may need. What they may need is different for each person. Some may need help getting out of a dangerous life, some may need help feeding their family, some may need clothes to keep them warm, and some may only need a kind word or a smile to brighten their day and give them hope.

As followers of His, and as servants of the kingdom, we have to get out of the pew, out of our boxes, and into the world. We have to ask for eyes to see, we need to ask for the power to change someone else's life. I can't tell you how to do that, you have to listen to what God is telling you, and then you need to do what He asks you to do. Then you have to trust Him to help you complete the task He has set before you.

God is going to call those who serve Him and do what He asks them to do when He returns, not those who sit in the pew once or twice a week and then don't do anything else. As a Christian your life should be reflecting the gifts you have received. You should be reflecting His love, joy, peace and mercy to a lost world. It's not just for a few to do, it's not just for missionaries in other countries, it is for each of us to be missionaries right here at home. We are all to show the light we have been given, a light so others can see their way in a dark world. It's not just for once in awhile, it's for every day.

Have a great day and God bless!

Challenge to be strong in trials

Good morning:

It is a cold morning here today. It has been a challenging 24 hours for many in the country and will continue to be for the next 24 to 48 hours. The storms that are causing so many problems across a vast portion of the U.S. are not finished yet. There are many who say that it is because of the pollution we have put in the atmosphere. I'm not going to try and dispute that claim, I am going to say what I believe. The earth is in one of its natural transformations. There have been times in past history, on our earth, when it has gone through similar transformations.

That said, the word persistence comes to mind today. Webster says persistence is to refuse to give up when faced with opposition; to continue insistently; to endure, to remain. Those going through the trials of heavy snow and ice across the nation today, along with very cold temperatures, find themselves having to be very persistent in their survival. That's what it comes down to in situations like this, persistence to survive and still maintain. Some will find they need help getting through the storms; others will suffer through it with no power; while others will persevere and even help those who need help.

A Christian's life is not a lot different, if we are to arrive at the place we want to be, that of being with Christ in eternity. We have to persist through all the trials of this world. Not only do we have to be persistent, never giving in to things, we have to show the rest of the world the love and grace we have been given through all of them.

> 1 Corinthians 13:4-7, "Love is patient, love is kind. It does not envy, it does not boast, it is not proud. It is not rude, it is not self-seeking, it is not easily angered, it keeps no record of wrongs. Love does not delight in evil,

but rejoices with the truth. It always protects, always trusts, always hopes, and always perseveres."

Now some of you are going to say, what does that have to do with today? The fact that we are to show love, patience, and kindness in our everyday walk means that even though we are meeting trials of frozen pipes, cold hands and feet, and no power, doesn't mean we cannot be persistent in our daily walk. It's the trials of life that cause us to grow and mature in Christ. We can't have a bad day and take it out on those around us. If we do, what does that say about our walk with God? Are others going to want to give up their pleasures in this world for something they don't see in us? They have to see us go through these trials, with the grace given us by Christ, for them to want to have what we have.

In Luke 8 Jesus is talking about the seed falling on different types of ground. He gives an explanation of what it means.

> Luke 8: 11-15, "This is the meaning of the parable. The seed is the word of God. Those along the path are the ones who hear, and then the devil comes and takes away the word from their hearts, so they won't believe and be saved. Those on the rock are the ones who receive the word with joy when they hear it, but they have no root. They believe for a while, but in the time of testing they fall away. The seed that fell among thorns stands for those who hear, but as they go on their way they are choked by life's worries, riches and pleasures, and they do not mature. But the seed on good soil stands for those with a noble and good heart, who hear the word, retain it, and by persevering, produce a crop."

Others need to see us go through the trials and how we handle them so they can determine how they will respond to the word of God. If we can go through them, depending on God, and not giving in to the pressures around us, others will see that it is worth the effort and the persistence for what is promised to us.

James 1:12, "blessed is the man who perseveres under trial; because when he has stood the test he will receive the crown of life that God has promised to them who love Him."

Have a great day and God bless!

Courage

Courage in faith

Good morning:

As I watched the birds taking flight this morning I remembered the Eagles I used to watch over the large lake up north. They are majestic birds; they have no fear of height and nest in the highest trees they can find. When they soar they are beautiful. I have often thought, watching them, how I would like to soar like that; to be able to look down on God's creation from on high, to fly above all the worldly commotion. To have the strength in the Eagles wings to soar like that would be wonderful.

Isaiah 40:28-31, "Do you not know? Have you not heard? The Lord is the everlasting God, the Creator of the ends of the earth. He will not grow tired or weary and His understanding no one can fathom. He gives strength to the weary and increases the power of the weak. Even youth grow tired and weary, and young men stumble and fall; but those who hope in the Lord will renew their strength. They will soar on wings like eagles; they will run and not grow weary, they will walk and not be faint." What a great verse, worth keeping handy.

There are days when we get up tired and feel like we have no strength. We get stuck here on earth and can't see the lofty heights that God wants us to see and feel. We are to trust Him and know He will be watching over us as we do His work.

The eagle takes off without a care, it trusts its maker and knows it will be able to fly with the strength it has been given. I wonder if we rise every morning, trusting and expecting that our strength is renewed. When we trust our Father with everything, we shouldn't need to worry about having what we need to get us through the day. Trusting in Him should give way to feeling His strength within us. Like the eagle God will give us the strength we need. He will also give us the ability to run the race and not get weary. To serve Him in all we do and to give Him the praise for what he has given us will bring us peace.

> 1 Peter 3:11, "He must turn from evil and do good; he must seek peace and pursue it."

I'm sure the eagle doesn't worry about anything; it just trusts and knows that everything it needs will be taken care of. It is at peace with the world around it.

My granddaughter asked today that I pray for her to have the strength to work with the people she has been given to take care of. Her new job is to be a home health nurse for terminal patients in their homes. What a wonderful way to serve God and others. What an opportunity to help them have peace during their last days.

Are we trusting as we should, are we pursuing peace, are we doing the things God has called us to do? He will give us the strength to do it, and even more.

Have a good day and God bless!

Courage as a Christian

Good morning:

Courage: Webster defines it as "a mental or moral strength to venture, persevere, and withstand danger, fear, or difficulty." Some think courage is the opposite of fear. Some think courage is doing something outstanding. Many think courage is what you either have or don't have in the face of danger. It's interesting to me to hear the different ideas people have about courage. Some feel they have no courage, some feel they have so much they can do anything and don't think about the consequences.

The book of Philippians was written by Paul while he was in a Roman prison. He was a follower of Christ and therefore despised by most in that time.

"Philippians 1:20, "I eagerly expect and hope that I will in no way be ashamed, but will have sufficient courage so that now as always Christ will be exalted in my body, whether by life or by death."

Paul was being faced with untold sufferings in prison. In a situation like that it can be easy to abandon your faith. Paul didn't know if he would live or die, but his prayer was that his courage would remain in Christ so that in life or death Christ would be exalted.

We face fear, anger, heartache, and suffering in our lifetime. Are we as concerned about how we face these challenges as Paul was? Are we concerned about how our response to these conditions affects others but most of all do we think about how our response portrays Christ to others? Too many times we just respond without thought of how others see it. If it feels good and if it sounds right and if we don't feel negative about it we think it is an ok response. We don't think about how God sees it, or if it's showing Him glory and honor. In those times our thoughts and responses are not on the things of heaven.

It takes courage to live as a Christian, to follow Christ's teaching, and go against the flow here on earth. It takes courage to say no to something others are asking us to do. It takes courage to say, I am going to church in the morning whether you go or don't go. It takes courage to not retaliate when we are hurt by others. It takes courage to stand up for what we believe to be true. It takes courage to stand up against a government that doesn't see any value in people or history or foundational truths. It takes courage to walk into the face of danger knowing what you are walking into. It takes courage to just live in this world today.

Courage is not the absence of fear, it is the strength to withstand it, and face the fear anyway. How do we find the strength to stand in the face of fear and danger? By setting up ideals for our lives that honor God and by knowing that in so doing He will be honored and will be there to give us the strength and courage to withstand whatever comes our way. To follow the two commands of Christ which cover all the other commandments.

> Matthew 22:37-40, "Love the Lord your God with all your heart and with all your soul and with all your mind. This is the first and greatest commandment. And the second is like it: Love your neighbor as yourself. All the Law and the Prophets hang on these two Commandments."

To live a life pleasing to Him and in all things, do it to honor Him. Do it because it will please Him and it will secure for you a place in eternity. Live your life with courage and strength because you have the power of the one who created the universe and who will, in the end, reign over all.

Have a great day and God bless!

Courage to move forward

Good morning:

Look at Romans 8:30-32 this morning, it will give you the courage to move on in your life. For many, each day is a trial, with many long hours to struggle through.

> Romans 8:30 -32; "And those he predestined, He also called, those He called, He also justified; those He justified, He also glorified. What, then, shall we say in response to this? If God is for us, who can be against us? He who did not spare his own Son, but gave him up for us all – how will He not also, along with Him, graciously give us all things"?

All sorts of things confront many of us, illness, loss of a job, death of friends or loved ones, bills that need paid, being hungry, or being homeless. These and other challenges in life burden us to the point that some of us think there is no hope, and they can't go any longer. Paul tells us in this verse, we are more than conquerors. God gave His supreme gift, His Son, to save us. He will certainly give whatever is necessary, to those who call Him Father, to deal with even the most challenging issues we face in life. Remember, even Paul pointed out in 2 Corinthians 2 that he had been shipwrecked, flogged, beaten, pelted with stones, suffered hunger and thirst, among a host of other sufferings. And God was with him and brought him through them all.

> Malachi 3:6, "I the Lord do not change. So you, O descendants of Jacob, are not destroyed. Ever since the time of your forefathers you have turned away from my decrees and have not kept them. Return to me and I will return to you, says the Lord Almighty".

God has not changed, He is always there, He has never misled anyone; He has never failed to fulfill His promises. Every day we meet challenges that can potentially divert us, and might even temporarily defeat God's purpose for our life.

Our life can sometimes be like the beaver and the dam. In the northwest, where I come from, we have lots of beaver. They are constantly building dams which are sometimes located in small streams. These dams often divert the main flow of water into a slightly different path. Sometimes they build on larger streams and the diversion causes problems downstream; someone has to go up steam and take care of the problem at the source. Sometimes they will choose a very large, very fast river and attempt to build their dams, and quite often their dams are washed downstream with the water. Then they rebuild and try to keep the dam in the same place. Life is like that, we can get diverted by a little incident and it can cause us to stray for a little while, but like the small stream it will eventually rejoin the larger flow a short distance downstream.

Sometimes we let things divert us and we don't correct it and it becomes a larger problem later on. It gets larger and spreads into other areas of our lives, and then we have to tackle where they started and get rid of them. Sometimes we let the little things become a big fast flowing river in our life. In those times, like the beaver, we can work all the time and not get anywhere, we have allowed Satan to come in and continually destroy what we have built so diligently. You see in the small stream the beaver lives a peaceful life, his dam has not caused too much trouble and the stream goes on. In the larger stream the dam has caused little damage right where it is, but downstream it creates lots of problems.

When we don't take care of things at the beginning they build into greater and greater problems. Now as the dam flows into the fast flowing river it doesn't allow the dam to stand very long. The swift current carries it away. We can work day and night and never get things completed. Life can be that way if we are not allowing God to be in control. Satan loves to keep us in turmoil all the time. We think we are getting ahead, and wham, the current hits us off we go just to have to start all over again. The only way to stop thist is to find a quieter place to build our dam. That place is in God's loving care.

Kay Ashwell

When we turn all these things over to God and let Him have control of them He can never be defeated. The storms of life may still be there, but God has them under control and we can depend on that. If our purposes are aligned with His, even though God's will in our life is temporarily diverted by our sin or mistakes, by circumstances, or even by the harm someone else inflicts on us, we can never be defeated as long as we are co-operating with God.

We have this as a promise:

> Romans 8:31-32, "What, then, shall we say in response to this? If God is for us, who can be against us; He who did not spare His own Son, but gave Him up for all of us, how will He not also, along with Him, graciously give us all things"?

> James 1:16-18, "Don't be deceived, my dear brothers, Every good and perfect gift is from above, coming down from the Father of the heavenly lights, who does not change like shifting shadows. He chose to give us birth through the word of truth; that we might be a kind of first fruit of all He created."

Be confident that He will keep His promise. Be patient, and let this truth light your way when it seems dark, God has not changed his mind concerning you, and He never will. He may allow you to wait in order to build your faith, but His promise will remain sure and true.

Stay in His care, if you stray a little let Him bring you back to the correct path, if things get bigger, address it where it started and take care of it, if the world just won't give you any peace and things are always torn up, find the quieter path that He can give you by giving everything over to Him and follow where He leads.

Have a great day and God bless!

Conflict

Conflict in understanding scripture

Good morning:

In Exodus God gave explicit commands about the temple and what was to happen every morning. We sometimes forget that the Old Testament has any merit in our lives today. We need to go back and read it, there are a lot of very good things in it, and they have meaning for us today. God gave the Levites specific orders for morning worship, the priests of the temple were chosen from the tribe of Levi. The high priest had to do these four things:

- Trim the lamps, making sure each oil cup of the menorah had sufficient oil and that the wicks were properly positioned.
- To burn sweet incense on the incense altar.
- To burn the fat of the "peace" offering.
- Once a week the "shew-bread" was replaced with 12 fresh loaves; representing the 12 tribes of Israel.

This ancient ritual may seem strange and of no use for us today, but let's see what it all means. This ritual involved all of the senses and the mind. The priest stood before the Lord for examination. Do we put ourselves before the Lord every morning for examination of our heart and mind? They need to be free and open for God to use as He intends every day.

The lamps symbolize the need for light. Are our lamps trimmed each morning so that we can see with spiritual eyes, or do we forget to give the day to the Lord?

The incense is a picture of our need to be filled with God's presence. Do we pray for God to be present in our everyday activities and do we ask Him to keep us in His will throughout the day, in all we do?

The *peace* offering indicates the need for peace with God and with our fellow man. Are our daily activities showing the peace God places in us for others to see or are we letting the little things in life keep us from showing this peace in what we do?

The shew-bread indicates our daily need for food. Not just physical food, but spiritual food as well. Are we getting into the word every morning so it can feed us with its wisdom or are we in the habit of forgetting it until later in the day? This ritual said then and says today: "We need you, God without you, we have no life, no wholeness, no meaning."

If you are like me and if you are honest with yourself and with God, you probably don't come before Him with all this in mind in the morning. I know mornings are tough, we get up, many times still tired from the night before, and rush into the day that is filled from dawn to dusk with things that need to get done. If there is one thing God has shown me during my time of healing, because He just kept telling me to rest, it is that our need for God in the morning is essential. He appointed me to write these daily thoughts and the only time I can successfully do them is early in the morning. I have to ask Him every day what thought do we have for today. If I wait till later in the day I can't think clearly, the day has already affected me. We are fresh in the morning and if we turn our thoughts to Him when we first arise, we have a clear mind for Him to give us the peace we will need for the day and we have already asked Him to guide our day.

We don't have rituals to follow in today's world, but we must come before the Lord with the same spirit of dependency and obedience. The day ahead of us is not ours. Our lives belong to Him and our day and what we accomplish is His and should glorify Him. Everything we need He will supply. Each day is His, just as we are His.

Have a great day and God bless!

Conflict with relationships

Good morning:

Relationships are difficult to manage regardless of whether they are a loved one, a family member, a good friend, or a work relationship. Life can get increasingly difficult at times. For some people it is more difficult than for others. Some circumstances require much more time to deal with than others. Some relationships are on shaky ground at all times and require constant care. Others are more relaxed and can be enjoyed on most levels. Some have to be dealt with on a different level, for instance at work, in those situations you only have to deal with them in a polite, pleasant manner and things go fine. Most relationships, for the most part, are based on joy and pleasure. Some are based on love, those can be both filled with joy and pleasure, but they can also cause us the most hurt. When this happens life can change for us quickly and become more difficult.

Things can turn quickly when we have been hurt, or taken a verbal beating, or been put down by some other force in our life. What happens when an angry word, a bad break, a new threat is thrown at us to fret over and we are suddenly in a struggle each day just to keep going? When those things come, and most will experience them at some time, we sometimes don't even want to get out of bed. What is there to get up for? What do I have to give to this crazy life? What good am I doing anyone?

The things we have to keep in mind, at all times, is that God is always there for us. He already knows that relationships are often hard to handle. He has given us many examples in Scripture of good relationships and not so good relationships. They can be beautiful and they can be challenging at the same time. But God understands all of them. David in the Psalms expresses these feelings quite well. He knew hardship, he knew difficult times, he knew times of rejection, but like Job, persevered through it all, he kept his heart and mind on the things of God. Paul, who was Saul, learned that life with Christ was hard, but satisfying, when lived for God in the manner of God's call.

Whenever we get angry, mad, or upset about our life we need to look at why it is causing us so much trouble. We should take into consideration everything that irritates us about others; it's our key to understanding who we are. What angers you, what upsets you, what makes you mad at another person is an unhealed aspect of yourself. If you had already resolved that particular issue in your life, you would not be irritated by its reflection back to you.

God sees us and our troubles in different ways than we see them. We see them with human eyes; He sees them and us with spiritual eyes. Jesus taught us how to look with Spiritual eyes, if we listened to Him and His messages. Life is going to bring us ups and downs; we need to just realize that fact. But we can have more ups than downs when we trust God with each one of them. God is on those ups and downs with us when we allow Him to have a part in our lives. When we let Him show us how to see others the way He sees them, and when we love others the way He loves them.

God understands relationships can be difficult; He uses those difficulties to make us stronger and to grow us into the kind of person He wants us to be. We can learn from the relationships we have, or have had, we can gain understanding through them, we can see them in a different way when we give them, and the situation to God to handle. He may ask us to do something about the relationship if it is one of anger, disappointment, or hurt but if we follow what He asks us to do in it; we will come through it with peace and with new and better understanding of ourselves and others.

Ask God to stand alongside you, to go before you in some relationships, to help you see with His eyes. Ask for His help in overcoming your anger, your frustration, your worry, your hurt over situations. Ask Him to let you see things in a different light, the light that He gives. Ask Him to show you how to get along with some situations; then hope the situation becomes right. Ask for wisdom, creative ways to approach each person and each situation, and patience to be able to deal with it. Ask Him to help you see, understand, accept, and love those we have relationships with.

> 1 Corinthians 13: 4-7 gives us the foundation on which to build these relationships: "Love is patient, love is kind. It does not envy, it does not boast, it is not proud. It is not rude, it is not self-seeking, it is not easily angered. It keeps no record of wrongs. Love does not delight in evil, but rejoices with the truth. It always protects, always trusts, always hopes, and always perseveres."

If we keep in mind that God is love, that He sees with eyes of love, that He wishes for all of us to see and love with the same eyes of love, then the relationships we have will only bring us joy and pleasure. We will also be bringing joy and pleasure to Him.

Ask God to help you love the way He loves, to see with the eyes He sees with. Ask Him to be in the middle of everything you do and say and you will find that your relationships will grow and mature and become more valuable to you and less frustrating.

Have a great day and God bless!

Conflict in daily situations

Good morning:

In conflicts there are two sides and each has to be addressed. To each side comes the belief that they are correct and that the other one is wrong. When talked over in a civil Christian conversation, they would probably find out that both sides were wrong. That neither was totally right and neither side was totally wrong.

Conflicts come about because pride gets in the way. Neither side can see the other person's viewpoint. They only see their side. Instead of discussing what each thinks, they do one of two things. First, one side believes they have everything figured out and know what has to be done and tells the other side what they need to do to correct it without hearing what the other has to say, or they just don't want to hear what the other feels because they already have determined they are correct.

Second, neither bothers to have a conversation regarding the conflict and they both go on feeling they are correct in their thinking. Both have a pride problem, as I see it. Neither wants to admit that they may have had a part in causing the conflict. They both feel they have been treated unfairly, they have been accused of something unfairly and it never gets straightened up and fixed, it just keeps causing more and more problems.

Poor communication, lack of self-control, lack of patience, lack of truly listening to what the other side has to say will cause untold damage to both sides. The sad thing is in most cases it is the unrecognized pride on both sides that has truly caused the problem. Confrontation is something that no one wants. But not being willing to bring up unpleasant situations thinking they will, in time, correct themselves is not healthy. The longer it goes unaddressed the more damage it does. People don't like to say I'm sorry, I didn't see your side of things. So they don't. They just continue to look at their side of the situation. Some in fact can't admit to being wrong.

Pride can come between family members, destroying family relationships. It can come between friends, causing good relationships to be destroyed in the process. It can be seen in the work place, causing untold damage to the business. It can be seen in nations, causing world tension or war. It can and is seen in most churches, causing a serious problem in the body.

The sad thing is in most cases; both sides truly care for the other side. But neither side is willing to have the conversation that could heal the whole situation. You see it in marriages, in family situations, in governments, in the business world, between friends, and unfortunately you see in the Christian community as well. Satan is having a field day with this one thing. He is content with what is happening, because it is causing problems for God's people. Satan's whole purpose is to cause division amongst God's people and destroy family units and cause nation to rise up against nation. The more he can keep people from facing the fact that they are prideful in their thinking the happier he is; especially when it comes to families and God's people. He tries to cause great divisions in these two areas particularly.

The other sad thing is unresolved conflict, pride, and trust that has been broken, is sin. Plain and simple, unresolved sin causes a separation between God and man. It doesn't matter who is right or wrong, it doesn't matter if you have been hurt, if the conflict has not been dealt with and is left open and hurting, it is sin on both sides. If it is still causing someone or several someone's to hurt, it has not been dealt with.

Sin that is taken care of, conflicts that are resolved are forgotten, the people can be at rest and at peace with it, but if there is no peace or rest regarding the situation it has not been fully addressed nor forgiven no matter how much you tell yourself it has.

Search your hearts today and if there are any unresolved conflicts in your life you need to take care of them, you need to ask God to show you what they were, be wiling for Him to tell you what you need to do, and then you must do it. Don't let hurts, misunderstandings, confusions, conflicts, pride, get in the way of the peace and reconciliation that can come from facing the fact that it takes two sides to cause a conflict.

Just as it takes two people to make a conflict, it takes both sides to make it right again. The longer it remains unresolved, the harder it is to take care of and the worse the situations will become. If a joint meeting can't be made, you need to take it to the Lord and ask Him to accept the fact that you have come to realize you had a part in it and that you are sorry for it. You have to keep yourself right with God. But you have to face the situation with an open mind, one that is not allowing pride to enter in. Satan is good at keeping that five letter word *pride* foremost in every situation. He will even make it seem like it is something else when in fact all it amounts to is the pride of thinking we are correct.

> Micah 6:8, "He has showed you, o man, what is good.
> And what does the Lord require of you? To act justly
> and to love mercy and to walk humbly with your God".

We are to walk humbly before God, to not look at our self more than we should; to truly forgive comes from the heart and not just something we think we have done. When we feel we have been wronged it has to be truly, honestly, and humbly forgiven. It has to come from a heart of love for Him and what He has shown us. We can't let Satan continually hammer us with it, but if it has not been honestly forgiven or dealt with, it needs to be.

Conflicts come into everyone's life, it's how we deal with them, and how we face them that make the difference in their resolution. Let God tell you what to do, then do it, whether you think it should be done or not. God does know best and if we are His child we have to listen to what He is saying.

Have a great day and God bless!

Faith

Faith in God's Word

Good Morning:

Faith and belief, are they the same? I don't think so; we can believe in everything that God has done, in all the beauty around us. We can believe that Christ died on the cross to save us from our sins. We can believe He still performs miracles' today. We can believe everything the Bible says. Sometimes we get caught in unbelief. Now don't tell me you have never doubted that God would get you out of a certain situation, or at least that you didn't see how He could. Well, that is unbelief.

Mark 9: 23; "All things are possible to him who believes."
Mark 9:24, "I do believe: help me overcome my unbelief."

So where does our Faith come into this? Faith is putting belief into action. If we believe all these things then we should have faith to act on them. Faith to know when He asks us to do something we can get it done. We have the power through faith to do anything we are asked. How often do we put that power and faith to work? It's so much easier to find an excuse to only do a partial job.

Luke 17: 5, "If you had faith like a mustard seed, you could say to this Mulberry tree, 'be uprooted and planted in the sea,' and it would obey you."

There is a story in 1 Kings 17 about a widow and her son who believed in the God of Israel, when asked by Elijah to bring him something to eat she replied I have only a little flour and oil, I am making a loaf for my son and myself and then we will lay down and die. Elijah told her first to make him a loaf of bread and bring it to him and then make something for the two of them.

1Kings 17:14, " For this is what the Lord of Israel says; The jar of flour will not be used up and the jug of oil will not run dry until the day the Lord gives rain on the land.."

The widow women did as she was asked, and was blessed!

Another story in 2 Kings 4 is about Elisha and a widow woman with 2 sons. Her husband was dead and they were going to come get her 2 sons and put them in bondage because of debts owed.

> 2 Kings 4: 3-7, Elisha replied to her, How can I help you? Tell me what you have in your house. Your servant has nothing there at all, she said, except a little oil. Elisha said, Go around and ask all your neighbors for empty jars. Don't ask for just a few. Then go inside and shut the door behind you and your sons. Pour the oi; into all the jars and as each is filled put it to one side. She left him and afterward shut the door behind her and her sons. They brought the jars to her and she kept pouring. When all the jars were full she said to her son; bring me another one. But he replied, There is not a jar left. Then the oil stopped flowing. She went and told the man of God, and he said, Go and sell the oil and pay your debts. You and your sons can live on what is left"

What about these two widows? It would have been easy for them to say, how can I do that when I only have enough for one meal for us? Both stories tell us they followed directions exactly. They had *faith* in the God of Israel, our God, and followed the directions of the prophets that God had sent to help them. That's the kind of faith we need to have. We can't do only half a job for the Lord, if He gives us something to do, He intends for us to carry it out as instructed, regardless of what that means for us.

God will not ask us to do something that He will not be there to see us through.

Kay Ashwell

Luke 17: 1-4, "Jesus said to his disciples; Things that cause people to sin are bound to come, but woe to that person through whom they come. It would be better for him to be thrown into the sea with a millstone tied around his neck than for him to cause one of these little ones to sin. So watch yourselves. If your brother sins, rebuke him, and if he repents, forgive him, and if he sins against you seven times in a day, and seven times comes back to you and says, I repent, forgive him."

The little ones, are children, new believers, and those who don't understand, are baby Christians, not grounded in scripture. So when God gives us a task we need to do the very best we can with faith to know God will see us through it.

We are being watched by others to see if our faith is strong and if we will continue in our faith whatever comes our way. If we hold fast and carry on they see faith in action; if however, we only do part of the job and let the rest of it go, they will see a weak faith and they won't hold much stock in it.

Faith is the thing this world is looking for, are we giving it our best where we are? Are Christians around the world doing the best they can or are we slacking off so the world can't see the faith we have? The mustard seed is the smallest seed, but grows into a large plant. Is our faith as strong as the mustard seed?

God bless and have a great day!

Faith when we worry

Good morning:

Let's see if I can start this week off better than last! We are on our property, after many challenging situations. We are fairly set for the time being, especially since I can do very little yet. Have things to get done but at least we are situated for now. In all the hassle of what had to get done, it became easy to let the negatives of this world creep into our lives. I think that is because we see what is before us with our eyes and feel the dreariness of it all. But we need to remember what Jesus said:

> John 20: 29, "Because you have seen me, you have believed. Blessed are those who have not seen and yet have believed."

As Christians who believe in our Lord and Savior we should never doubt that He is there with us, even going before us, to prepare the way. We need to awake every day with the focus that He is in control of our every move. We can do nothing on our own so why do we even try.

As I sit here and look out my window and see God's creation all around me I cannot fail to see the flowers, trees, birds, butterflies, and yes even the ants, (which try to invade my home), trust that they will be taken care of. They come to life on time, every day and don't worry about anything. We need to do the same. Trusting is the essence of faith. The birds have faith that they will find food, will have a tree to rest in, the flowers will burst into beautiful color each year. As Christians we trust that scripture is the Holy word of God, if we trust that He loves us and we trust that He has forgotten our past sins, and we trust that He is going to lead us forward in the path He has chosen for us, then this is Faith. We need to awake each morning with the faith that creation has. Faith to know that there is nothing that God can't handle.

Kay Ashwell

We need to remember that He doesn't want us to worry or fret, they impede our growth. We need to give Him our fears and doubts each day and let Him carry them while we enjoy where we are and what He has done for us. We need to allow God to care for us, just as He cares for the rest of His creation. He wants for us to be free from the worries of the world, to be free of doubts, to be free to love and praise Him each day. So each morning let us draw nearer to God by giving Him our day and our lives. Life will be much easier when we do. There is nothing that He can't handle; after all He created this world and all that is in it.

1 Peter 5:7, "Cast all your anxiety on him because he cares for you."

Just as He cares for the birds of the air and the flowers in the field, He cares for and loves each and every one of us.

He wants to carry those worries and doubts the world throws at us. He wants us to be free to worship Him and enjoy what He has given us. He wants us to have fun watching His world and how He will take care of things. He wants us to share His creation with others so they too can be free of the world.

Have a great day and God bless!

Faith in darkness

Good Morning:

Each morning as I sit here I watch the darkness of night slowly turn to the light of day. When I arise the world outside is dark except for some spots of light here and there. In those spots of light I can see what is out there. Where there is no light I can't make out anything but shadows.

People's lives are like that. They live in a world of darkness where they can't see how to take the next step. They are a prisoner of darkness; it holds them in the spot they are in. They can't see where to step next so they just stay right where they are. They continue to do the same things because they don't know how to do anything else. Once in awhile someone will see a spot to light in the distance and will be brave enough to try to reach it so they can see where they are going.

The darkness around them tries to keep them there because it doesn't want them to get to the light. It has logs, ditches and holes for them to get caught in along the way. Some will never make it to the light because they become weak and tired of all the obstacles in their way, it's easier to just stay where they are. Some will battle their way to just outside the light and give up, they are too tired to go on. They need a rest and so they remain just outside the light. They see just a little but don't have the courage trust, and power to make it any farther. There are some who make it into the light and find that life looks a lot different when they are in the light. They can see where they are going, where the path is so they move from light to light with the faith they have found.

Jesus is the light source for the world. He offers love, strength, hope and power to keep moving into the light of His eternal care. He has given each of us the ability to have faith in His love. He has given us the way to meet every challenge of life. He has also given us the responsibility to reach out into the darkness and give a helping hand to those just outside the light and give them a hand to come into the light. To some He has given the responsibility of going out into the darkness to find those who are too afraid to leave the darkness because they don't have the faith to traverse the obstacles in their way.

Those of us who have been given the power to overcome the darkness have a daily responsibility to guide others into the light. Sometimes this is easy because some are just waiting to be given a hand, for others it is more difficult because first they have to be given the knowledge and see the trust that God is offering them. Once they come to understand the love and peace that awaits those who come into the light they will follow you back into the light of God.

Some, I'm sorry to say, will never find their way into the light because they like what the darkness is offering them. They like to stay where they are; it's easier than finding the light. They just keep doing what they want and don't want to have to change; they are familiar with their life and have no power or desire to change it. To those we can only keep calling out to, and ask them to come toward the light and let us help them find it. We may never see them come into the light, but someone else might. We can never quit calling into the darkness of this world to those who don't what to live in the light.

Jesus is the light that keeps us. He is the light that radiates out and beckons all to come into His light. Some come easy, some come with lots of difficulty and some never will come. We, who know the light, can't take the easy path and just move about in the light. We have to reach out into the darkness and grab hold of someone and bring them in with us. Many are waiting for that helping hand, the one that they can trust and take hold of to help them come in. We have to be willing to try to find them and show them the way.

Jesus didn't just sit and let the people come to Him, He was always moving about, bringing them to Himself. He was always reaching out to the lost and lonely, the downtrodden and the unwanted. We must do the same if we are to be called one of His.

Have a great day and God bless!

Faith in the Scriptures

Good morning:

The sun is out today and the sky is blue. There is a light breeze and the earth is refreshed from the rain. Fall is definitely here and winter won't be far behind. Planting in Texas is new to me, but I am told I need to plant the Blue Bell seeds in the fall. So I think I will do that today. This brings to mind the scripture of the farmer and the seeds that Jesus talked about in Luke 8.

I remember driving on back roads in Idaho in the summer and fall and noticing all the plants that were growing outside the fields. They grow a lot of wheat and oats so they were easy to pick out. Some were so choked with weeds in the ditches they could hardly be seen. Some of the others were along the edge of the road in the gravel and they just weren't growing at all. The fields were different also; some were full of weeds and wild flowers, along with the grain. Some fields were full with tall, healthy spikes of wheat or oats.

It was just like the story in Luke 8: 5-15. Some of the seeds the farmer sowed fell among the rocks and did not grow, like some people that hear and see God in others but just can't grasp the fact that they need Him. They continue to go about their day as always and carry all the troubles and trials on their own with no help, some won't even think of asking for help. They just struggle along from day to day.

Some of the seeds fell in the ditch, where there is some nourishment, some water, but no care. Like people who come to church once in awhile, who may open their Bibles once or twice a year, who can recognize their need for a heavenly father, but who never get interested enough to follow through with Him. They seem to think that if they get a little now and then it will be enough to carry them through the tough times.

Then there are the fields which have been planted but not cared for. These are the people who come to church quite regularly, but who don't get involved in anything that is going on. They just don't have time to participate in Bible studies, they don't join in any of the ministries of the church, they are just waiting for someone to give them what they think they deserve. They will never produce a good clean life just as that field will not produce a good clean crop. They will be lukewarm people just warming a seat in a church.

Then there is the field that has been taken care of, the one that is producing a good clean crop. These are the people who have committed themselves to the Lord. They are the ones who do what the Lord is asking them to do. They are the ones who lead others, strengthen others. They are the ones that others look to for help. They are the producers because they know where their help and strength and power come from. They depend on Him every day to guide and direct them.

When we plant the way the Lord expects us to, we will have a good crop; one that will grow each day, one that will produce the fruit that He expects and the one that will have a plentiful harvest.

Which one are you? Do you plant but don't follow through? Do you just scatter seeds and let them grow on their own? Do you plant the seed with love, water it and care for it as it grows?

The crop the Lord is looking for is the one that is cared for, the one that is producing, the one that knows where it's food, water, strength, and power comes from; the one that gives Him control everyday knowing that He cares for it and will keep the weeds and rocks out.

Each of us should be striving to be the field that is clean, productive and strong. One that can stand the winds that will come. I pray that each of you are or will seek this kind of field.

Have a good day and God bless!

Faith in God's promises

Good morning:

Election Day is over, the day is again dreary, but there is hope in the air. The leaves are standing tall and firm, even with the golden hue they now hold. The plants are absorbing the moisture into their roots. The grass is looking greener. Yes there is hope in the air.

As I was studying for my Sunday school class, we are still in Genesis, and reading about Abraham and the promises God made with him, I realized that no matter what happens today, God has already got it handled.

There are some real positive things we can take from Abraham. He had the faith to answer God's call into unknown territory. He gave up everything we find so comforting today; His home, his family, his identity; to do what? Follow God's direction into a new land where no one would know him. In those days that was dangerous. But He had the faith in God to know that he would be all right.

Lessens, we can lean from him, are that even with faith there are trials. Being a Christian doesn't take the trials away; the greater the faith, the greater the trials. Take away the trials and where is our faith? Faith must be tried, in order that faith may live and grow. If the son of God had trials why shouldn't we? The key question is: do we have the faith to carry us through the trials that we face? Do we look to God for the answers or do we just march along to the music and do what comes natural, what seems right? We learn patience and meekness through these trials. When we ask for assistance in solving them God is loving and gracious to give us the peace to know that all will be ok.

> I John 2:17, "The world and its desires pass away, but the man who does the will of God lives forever."

When we have faith regardless of the trials, when we call on Him for answers, when we pray 'thy will be done', and mean it, we are in the will of God. When we pray, 'thy will be done', we are humbling ourselves before our Lord. It shows a willing, loving heart, one that the Spirit can live in.

> Isaiah 41:10; "So do not fear, for I am with you; do not be
> dismayed, for I am your God. I will strengthen you and
> help you: I will uphold you with my righteous right hand."

A promise to the Israelites, a promise for us today; we just need the faith to follow His guidance.

Yes, there is hope, there is hope for a new tomorrow, a hope that only a soul that lives for God will understand. No matter what tomorrow may bring, no matter what the rest of today will bring, God gives us hope, peace, love, and the understanding to know who we can depend on. Jesus is our friend, our brother and our savior. What better hope is there than this? Our lives are not remembered in stone monuments, but how we touch the people we are entrusted with. That is our calling; it is what God is expecting us to do. Touch someone else's life. Give someone else the peace we have. Today our country is standing on the edge of a new beginning, and we are standing on the edge of a new day. Lift someone up; they may be standing on the edge of a cliff.

Look around; someone is in need of a smile, a kind word, a prayer, a positive motive to continue. Let us run with perseverance the race set before us. We know the end, others out there don't. Let our legacy be one that, when we meet our maker.

> Matthew 25:23, "Well done, good and faithful servant.
> You have been faithful with a few things; I will put you
> in charge of many things. Come and share your master's
> happiness."

The lives we touch may be forever changed by what we say and do. Some of them reach out and hurt us, some of them we tolerate, some of them we love, but remember no matter whom that person is, God wants to redeem them.

The best relationship is not the one that brings together perfect people, but the best is when each individual learns to live with the imperfections of others and can admire the other person's good qualities. In other words, learn to love the negative people in your life. It will please God and bring peace and joy to your soul.

Have a good day and God bless!

Faith in God's love

Good morning:

Paul, in Romans 5:1-11 explains the result of living by faith in a right relationship with God. Paul is consistent in all his letters in how he links faith, hope, love and joy together. When he mentions one he usually mentions the others. That's because they go together. As you have probably already noticed I say much the same thing in my daily thoughts; they are the messages God gives me, the messages must be important.

The book of Romans is a book on Faith. In these verses Paul brings the *hope* of the gospel to the people. The good news that came with Jesus is one of hope, love, joy, and peace which all come through Faith in Christ Jesus, our Savior. Paul, in writing to the Roman Jews, and us, wants them and us to understand that they can't have these other things until and unless there is *faith in Jesus*, and why He came to earth to die for us on the cross.

In today's world many Christians have heard it so much they don't recognize it as *good news*. We have come to take it as an expected part of life. The fact is we should treat it as good news every day. It should be taken as a precious gift, not as an expected result. We should never get to the point in our Christian walk when we feel that our salvation is secure. It is only secure when we continually keep Christ and His wishes for our life in the front of each new day. If we are truly His, each day should be looked at as a gift given to us for carrying out His desires and plans for our lives. We should never take God's love for granted. His love is forever and the hope it gives us will never disappoint us. But we can never take it for granted. When we start to expect it, to take it for granted we have stopped letting Him have control of our life and we have become our own god.

Romans 5:8-11, "But God demonstrates His own love
for us in this: While we were still sinners, Christ died

for us. Since we have now been justified by His blood, how much more shall we be saved from God's wrath through Him! For if, when we were God's enemies, we were reconciled to Him through the death of His Son, how much more, having been reconciled, shall we be saved through His life! Not only this, but we also rejoice in God through our Lord Jesus Christ, through whom we have now received reconciliation."

Christ's death on the cross is the basis for our justification, and therefore our reconciliation with God. Some don't understand the meaning of justification, in the time that the Romans were in power, to be justified was a strong word and held a great deal of meaning. In their legal system, the person who was acquitted of a crime, it meant that all charges were dropped, their criminal record was erased. They were set free.

Think about that for a minute. When the crowd set Barabbas free, even though he was a very bad person, they forgave his crimes; he was a free man. While Jesus, an innocent person, died in his place on the cross. He died for every sinner. Because of His obedience to God and His love for each sinner, we are no longer hopeless sinners. We were guilty of our sins, but He wiped them away over two thousand years ago. Because we have chosen to follow His word, to model after His life we have been shown mercy and our sins are no more. *We have been set free.*

So why do we think we can take His love and forgiveness for granted? We should be thankful every minute of every day that we are loved that much. We should never take it for granted. It is a free gift we should cherish every day. We should be showing our love, in return, to others just as Christ did for us. Our trials are to bring us to greater understanding, for through our trials, and our sufferings, we learn perseverance, perseverance produces character, and character hope, and hope does not disappoint us; this can be found in Romans 5: 5-8.

Our Faith in Christ brings the hope; the hope brings love, joy, and peace. We cannot take those things for granted! They are the things which

Kay Ashwell

will sustain us in times of grief, in times of hurt, in times of confusion. Our Faith in Christ is hope, the hope for a life of freedom, which we should not take for granted. But should be praising and thanking Him for all the time. It should always be *good news* to us. We should never get apathetic about it.

Churches and Christians today have gotten very apathetic, taking for granted the love and mercy and hope that has been given to us. God is trying to get our attention, are we listening? I pray we are, because He will be coming soon to take those who are ready out of this world. Are you ready? Have you asked for your sins to be forgiven, it's a daily necessity you know? Have you given your life to Him for guidance and control? Are you doing what He has asked you to do or are you fighting it?

It's not too late; you just have to sincerely ask Him for forgiveness, ask Him to come into your life and clean it up and keep it clean. He is faithful to forgive us our sins when we allow Him control of our life. It can and will be a life of love, joy, peace and hope. They are inseparable when He is in control. They are what He is. What more could you want in this life, but hope, love, joy and peace? It's all there when you have *faith and trust* in our Lord and Savior.

Have a great day and God bless!

Fear

Good day:

This thought is not one of the original ones God gave me several years ago. This one He has given me just recently in March 2020.

The Corona Virus is running rampant around the world. People in this country are going crazy buying up everything they think they may need. They are buying out of *fear*. Fear of the unknown is driving this buying; even people who have claimed to be Christians for a long time are caught up in the fear.

Fear is not from God, it is a trick of Satan. Yes, we are all going through testing right now. Testing is to determine our *faith* it has two outcomes. We can trust our Lord to give us the peace to stay the course and let others know there is a difference in us by our actions. Or the other outcome is those who don't know Him let the unknown control their thinking as they live in fear. We are given a life of *hope* through the resurrection of Christ from death.

It was during this time I lost my husband, on March 14; Our Lord took him home. My friend and pastor sent me:

> 1 Peter1: 5-9, "who through faith are shielded by God's power until the coming of the salvation that is ready to be revealed in the last time. In this you greatly rejoice, though now for a little while you may have had to suffer grief in all kinds of trials. These have come so that your faith of greater worth than gold, which perishes even though refined by fire – may be proved genuine and may result in praise, glory, and honor when Jesus Christ is revealed. Though you have not seen Him, you love Him; and even though you do not see Him now, you believe in Him and are filled with an inexpressible

and glorious joy, for you are receiving the goal of your faith, the salvation of your soul."

There is no place for fear in a believer's life. The faith of a believer should be stronger than any fear Satan tries to instill in humanity. God has power over any storm. When we fix our eyes on Him it leads to peace, even when we walk through a new valley. A couple of Scriptures has led Don and I, through many valleys of unknown situations. I am now walking a new valley and we are all walking new unknowns.

Psalm 23: 4; "Even though I walk through the valley of death, I will fear no evil, for you are with me; your rod and thy staff they comfort me."

The valley of death is any trial or change we don't know the way through. The rod and staff is His gentle guidance through it just as a shepherd guides his sheep. Then we have the promise God gave to Joshua when he was getting ready to lead the Israelites into the Promised Land.

Joshua 1: 9;"Have I not commanded you? Be strong and courageous. Do not be terrified; do not be discouraged, for the Lord your God will be with you wherever you go."

Matthew 8 tells of a time when Jesus and the disciples were in a boat in the middle of the Sea of Galilee. Jesus was sleeping and a large wind came up and the disciples were afraid. Jesus wakes and asks:

Matthew 8: 26; "You of little faith, why are you so afraid?"

Christians need to remember God has power over every storm. In the middle of the storm when the wind and waves seem to overwhelm us we shouldn't let them cause fear. We may not be able to change the situation, but we can choose to faithfully trust God in the middle of it.

We need to fix our eyes on Jesus and find peace. We can't look at the size of the storm, but turn to the One who can calm it. Only by focusing on God who knows every outcome, can we navigate through any situation with His wisdom and peace.

Jesus is always with us. It is easy to focus on the fears when you have no control over the future. Jesus thankfully knows our future and He is always by our side, or perhaps carrying us through it. He calls us to live by faith, trusting in Him and not by fear or what we see with earthly eyes; you of little faith, why are you afraid?

> Haggai 2: 4b-5; "be strong, all you people of the land," declares the Lord, "and work. For I am with you, declares the Lord. This is what I covenanted with you when you came out of Egypt. And my Spirit remains among you. Do not fear."

I need to stop here for a moment; Haggai is speaking to the people of God, the Israelites. For us today since the resurrection of Jesus, those who believe in Him and call Him savior, turn over their lives, are Israelites; we belong to the family of God. We are among the chosen; we have the same promises.

> 2 Corinthians 3:17; "Now the Lord is the Spirit, and where the Spirit of the Lord is, there is freedom."

Freedom my friends, we need not fear.

Christians need to be confident in their faith. Earth is not our home; we are only here for a little while. We are to show others how to be free, how to have peace and joy in their life. One day we will be in our home with our Lord for eternity.

> 2 Corinthians 5:5-7; "Now it is God who has made us for this very purpose and has given us the Spirit as a deposit guaranteeing what is to come; therefore we are always confident and know that as long as we are at home in the body we are away from the Lord. We live by faith, not by sight."

The body it is referring to in this verse is our earthly body.

We have to persevere in life; the Holy Spirit of God dwells with us, reminding us of what is to come, *everlasting life.* Ask the Spirit and He will give you the perseverance and the power to overcome anything you face. He will give you the power to finish the race here on earth.

> 2 Timothy 1:13-14; "What you hear from me, keep as the pattern of sound teaching. With faith and live in Christ Jesus. Guard the good deposit that was entrusted to you— guard it with the help of the Holy Spirit who lives in us."

I would ask you to read Psalm 91; it is not too long, but it is a Psalm of hope for everyone. It is too much to write it all here, but I want you to remember

> Psalm 91: 2-6; "I will say to the Lord, He is my refuge and my fortress, my God, in whom I trust. Surely He will save you from the fowler's snare and from the deadly pestilence. He will cover you with His feathers, and under His wings you will find refuge, His faithfulness will be your rampart. You will not fear the terror of night; nor the arrow that flies by day; nor the pestilence that stalks in the darkness; nor the plagues that destroy at midday".

> Psalm 91: 9-10; "If you make the most High your dwelling – even the Lord who is my refuge – then no harm will befall you, no disaster will come near your tent."

Yes, it is a Psalm of *hope.* He is my refuge and my fortress, my God, in whom I trust.

Don't be afraid, turn to God, He is ultimately in charge. If you haven't accepted Christ as your savior now would be the time to pray and ask God to forgive your sinful life, ask Jesus into your life as your savior and find the peace He has to offer you.

God bless you!

Forgiveness

Forgiveness toward others

Good morning:

> Romans 12:18 "Do your best to live at peace with everyone," and Romans 12:20-21 "If your enemy is hungry, feed him, if he is thirsty, give him something to drink. In doing this, you will heap burning coals on his head. Do not be overcome by evil, but overcome evil with good."

So what does all that mean to us? It means we should show those who do an injustice to us an attitude of forgiveness. When we do something good to someone who has wronged us they have to stop and consider why we would do that instead of taking revenge. In doing so they have to stop and consider why we would be nice and forgiving. It may even bring them to a place of repentance. But beyond that, such actions have the effect of overcoming evil with good. When we respond in love and forgiveness to evil, Satan has to take a back seat. If on the other hand we respond in anger, discouragement, or negativity we are allowing evil to enter into our lives as well. Jesus never got even with those who rejected and did evil to Him. Even on the cross Christ said:

> Luke 23:34a," Father; forgive them; for they do not know what they are doing."

There will be people in our lives who, no matter how accommodating and nice we may be, will never return our friendship. No matter how much we do for them, try to accommodate their needs, or just be nice to them, they are continually negative toward us. As Christians we have to continue to be nice to them and treat them with kindness, and eventually one of two things will happen. They will either come under conviction and change their attitude, or God will tell you that you no longer have a responsibility to them. We do not have to surrender our principles, we simply stand on them with gentleness and wisdom. Wisdom we get from our heavenly Father.

The only way to change the attitude of your rivals is by prayer; prayer and the understanding that God will do a work in their hearts. He is using us and our faith and trust in Him to cause them to look at what they are doing.

When negativity is met with positivity at all times, it will eventually cause others to face the truth. This is called enabling grace.

God has given us His peace, His grace, and His wisdom to be positive in these situations. We are the ones who are positive and that attitude will show through us at all times if we are willing to submit ourselves to the Lord.

At this time in the world Christians are being put to the test. But we have the promise from our Father that we can be strong and overcome the evil around us. Paul tells the Thessalonians, who are undergoing great tribulation, but to stand firm in their faith, believing the truth for their salvation.

We see false teachers, worldliness, and apathy in our everyday lives. But our responsibility is to stand firm in our faith and to believe the truth.

> II Thessalonians 2:15 –17; "So then brothers, stand firm and hold to the teachings we passed on to you, whether by word of mouth or by letter. May our Lord Jesus Christ Himself and God our Father, who loved us and by His grace gave us eternal encouragement and good hope, encourage your hearts and strengthen you in every good deed and word."

Yes, we have the hope and the promise that good will prevail and He is asking us to stand firm in our faith with positive responses to those negative ones that we encounter each day; stand firm, stand together.

Have a great day, God bless!

Kay Ashwell

Fruit of the Spirit

Fruit of the Spirit Components

Good morning:

> Galatians 5:22, " But the fruit of the Spirit is love, joy, peace, patience, kindness, goodness, faithfulness, gentleness and self control."

These don't come to us all at once. They build on one another. When we become a believer we have been given the love and the joy of the Father. Peace comes into our lives as we learn His love for us and we don't have to worry as the world does.

Patience is easier to accomplish when we have the other three in place. Patience is a continual process for most of us. When we think we have it God says oh, but I want you to have a little more. Without patience and the first three we would not be able to show kindness to others. One of the things others see is our kindness of the Spirit, which is so needed in this world today.

Goodness, what is that? Being a good person or doing good acts for others. I believe that in this case it is being able to do good things for others, especially those around us. It is easy to do that with our family, but it is not so easy to do it for others who have wronged us or are in the world. Without the love and joy of the Father, the peace we feel and the kindness we have learned there is no way we are going to exhibit this fruit of the Spirit.

Faithfulness is a twofold fruit, it is most importantly being faithful to our Lord who has given us everything, but it is also faithfulness in our responsibilities to our spouse, our church and other brothers and sisters, but also to the tasks God has given us to do. Don't forget faithfulness to self.

Gentleness, when we have gained and understand all the fruit of the spirit in front of this one it is easy to be gentle with people. It is important that we show and deal with others in and out of the church with gentleness. Christ was gentle in all He said and did, except when He was angry over the money changers who had invaded the temple. To the world and His friends and disciples He showed, faithfulness, goodness, patience, and love.

Self Control, oh boy, this is the last one and probably the hardest for us to grasp. I can tell you from experience if I didn't have the rest of the fruits I would not have self control. It is a matter of taking control of what we say, do, think, act and it needs to be seasoned with all the rest. The world is watching us and we need to not only put on God's armor daily, we need to keep the fruit of the Spirit always in the forefront of our minds.

Remember we are watched by other Christians as well as the world. Be kind, everyone you meet is carrying a heavy burden. Jesus treated everyone, even those against Him, with compassion. The world gives everyone enough burdens to deal with. We need to give them a taste of the fruit which comes with loving our Lord. Let us try, as we meet others, to show them love, as our Lord has shown love to each of us.

I think that we need to always show the joy we have in knowing Jesus. The world sees joy differently than we do. Joy to the world depends on external influences. We have the internal joy of knowing what lies ahead because we are part of the family of God. Joy is to be a way of life for believers.

1 Thessalonians 5:16; "Be joyful always."

Let's try to show this joy to the world, being a Christian is fun, let's enjoy the ride.

Psalm 33:22, "May your unfailing love rest upon us, O Lord, even as we put our hope in you."

God bless and have a great day!

Grace

Grace given by God

Good morning:

It's mid September, kids are back in school and nature is getting ready for the winter season. In the northwest at this time of year you see all sorts of things changing, the leaves turning beautiful colors, the hills are a vast palette of color, and the fields are either harvested or being harvested. The pumpkin fields seem to light up with an orange glow. These are the signs that God is preparing His creation for a period of renewal; a time when it gathers strength and renews its purpose.

What does our life look like? Are we being renewed each day or are we just sitting here absorbing what we want and leaving the rest? Is our life like an old car just sitting around gathering dust and taking up space? Or is it like the old car that some loving person has taken and brought back to life with waxing and polishing? You know to restore an old car to its beautiful state takes a lot of work. It takes pounding, sanding, painting, waxing and polishing. Similarly, that's what has to happen in our lives for them to be a light for others to see. God works this miracle in our lives when we allow Him to have control.

> 1 Corinthians 15:10, "But by the grace of God I am what I am, and this grace to me was not without effect."

We are to be examples of God's love to the world. He carefully restores us to become the type of person He wants us to be. He has called us out of the world and into His family. He wants and expects us to be like Jesus, a servant for His kingdom. We have been given grace by His forgiving heart. He has called us to be servants for Him.

> 1 Corinthians 4:1-2, "People should think of us as servants of Christ, the ones God has trusted with His secrets. Now in this way those who are trusted with something valuable must show they are worthy of that trust."

Ouch! Does our life show God's grace? Are we in the process of being restored or just taking up space?

Our lives should show His grace in what we say and do. God transformed Saul from a rigid Pharisee to a missionary with grace woven throughout his life. God made a new person in Paul, but Paul went through persecutions, shipwrecks, stoning, prison and more to mold him into the person most useful for God's purposes.

When we allow God to remake us, to restore us, it hurts, and is at best uncomfortable. But by His grace we are becoming what are most effective for His use. Are we effective in our walk? Are we using the grace God has given us to shine in someone else's life?

> Matthew 15:29; "To those who use well what they are given, even more will be given, and they will have an abundance."

Are we using well the gifts and talents God has given us? We need to be sure of where we are and what we are showing others in our daily walk. The world is in need of the grace God has to offer, they need to see grace being used by His people. We are being watched. Is what they see what God wants them to see?

We need to be positive; God's grace is an unmerited favor, but that grace also gives us the ability to do God's work.

> 2 Peter 1:3 -4; "His divine power has given everything we need for life and godliness through our knowledge of Him who called us by His own glory and goodness. Through these He has given us His very great and precious promises, so that through them you may participate in the divine nature and escape the corruption in the world caused by evil desires."

As we grow in His nature, goodness, knowledge, self-control, perseverance, godliness, brotherly kindness and love will work progressively to keep us from being ineffective and unproductive in our knowledge of our Lord and the way we should be living.

2 Peter 1:2: "Grace and peace be yours in abundance through the knowledge of God and of Jesus our Lord."

Today choose to be effective and productive as a participant in God's nature and revel in His abundant grace, letting His light shine through us before others.

May you have peace today and may that peace give you the desire to share it with someone else.

Have a great day and God bless you!

Grace in daily living

Good morning:

It's quiet in my house this morning so I can concentrate on God and what He is saying! The pressures of the day and the things that have to get done, the trials of trying to figure out what we should do, the stress of just living from one day to the next, the frustration of not being able to do something we want to do or need to do and the hurts we endure from friends and family can overwhelm us to the point we forget God's promises for us.

> Romans 8:18; "I consider that our present sufferings are not worth comparing with the glory that will be revealed in us."

God uses all of these things for good, to teach us character, patience, humility and faith. It is the achievement of His plan and the splendor of His presence with us that He freely shares with us. Impossible situations are God's specialty. We feel sometimes that if anything could go wrong it will. Remember that nothing is too difficult for God. We can have patience during these times of difficulty knowing that everything we perceive as obstacles in our path are nothing at all to God.

> Jeremiah 32:17; "Ah, Sovereign Lord, you have made the heavens and the earth by your great power and outstretched arm! Nothing is too hard for you."

God also wants us to remember the blessings He bestows upon us. His mercy and compassion are cause for praise. His approval and blessings are like being nourished from the springs of living waters. He rules heaven and earth but He cares for each of us individually. He knows our deepest hopes, and gives us tranquility in the midst of the storms of life.

> Numbers 6:24-26; "The Lord bless you and keep you, the Lord make His face shine upon you and be gracious

to you; the Lord turn his face toward you and give you peace."

This is God's blessing; It is the light that God shines in each of our hearts.

When times get rough or we go into that *pity party* mode, remember that God is on the throne and He is in control and He has the answers. Just turn to Him and praise Him for the joy and peace He puts in our hearts, minds and lives when we turn our face to Him.

Have a great day and God bless!

Grace in times of distress

Good morning:

We got rain last night and the curled up leaves of yesterday have uncurled and are still there, there is hope for the seemingly dead. Though some may yet fall, we may be able to see some saved. This is what our savior expects us to do. When we see the toll this world has on many it is our responsibility to give them hope and encouragement. Even when it may even seem to be a lost cause.

God's grace has given us the peace and faith to carry on in times of stress, confusion, disorder, and pain. Many in the world today don't have this peace. They are angry, but don't know why. Anger irritates, anger isn't easily silenced, and anger will increase and leave a person without any peace or hope. A person lost is one who only thinks of revenge, getting even, taking what they want no matter the cost. A person without God can't see a better future, so why try. So they become angry at everything and everyone, it becomes like a cancer eating away at the very soul of the individual. Oh, they can carry on as if nothing is wrong, but they will become more suspicious with each incident, and angrier at life.

It reminds me of the story of Joseph and his brothers, Genesis 37-50. His brothers were angry at Joseph for being the *special* child, angry at being second best to the youngest, angry, if it were told, at their father for his favoring of Joseph. They were just angry and so they sold him to gypsies and told their father he was dead. They were getting revenge, but revenge on whom?

> Hebrews 10: 30-31, "For we know him who said, it is mine to avenge; I will repay, and again, The Lord will judge his people. It is a dreadful thing to fall into the hands of the living God."

Kay Ashwell

So to me they didn't think their God could handle the situation. They just didn't think, because their anger was so deeply embedded in them they couldn't think, they could only get revenge.

God had other plans; he turned their anger and revenge into something good. He kept Joseph and Joseph kept the Lord, even through all the trials and hardships he endured. When the time came, instead of being angry at his brothers, he took them in and fed and clothed them. Even though Joseph showed no anger toward them, the brothers were still suspicious. So when their father died they went to Joseph and told him a lie, they said in Chapter 50, Your father has given this command before he died...Tell Joseph to forgive you.

Now Joseph could have gotten very angry with them, but he didn't. I love his response. He answered them,

> Genesis 50:19-20, "But Joseph said to them, don't be afraid. Am I in the place of God? You intended to harm me, but God intended it for Good to accomplish what is now being done, the saving of many lives."

Joseph had forgiven them years before; he was following the Lord and answered only to Him. Joseph knew the joy of peace and hope that comes through forgiveness. Forgiveness doesn't mean the person or persons that hurt you were right, it means letting God do what is right, it means letting God do the judging.

So what does this have to do with a curled up leaf that didn't fall during the night, but got refreshed with the rain? It is like anger, if we don't let go of it and seek revival through nourishment we will die, but if we take the pathway to revival things start to get better. The leave got revived by the rain. We get revived in trusting God.

We are God's nourishment for man on earth. We have been given the life sustaining water to keep us refreshed. We are to share it with others who need nourishment. We are the light which God has given the world. We have to accept that role and give nourishment, not anger to the dying world.

Do you think it is too big a job? I don't think so, where is the faith we have received? Where is the grace that has been given to us? We can't save the whole world at once, but we can start right here at home. We can show someone every day the love which we have been given. We can give it to someone who is curling up and withering.

We can let God handle the big stuff, we just need to be concerned about the situations He has put in our path today.

Have a good day and God bless!

Graciousness
in Speech

Good morning:

I have been thinking about this for a couple of days now. As you know our granddaughter has just recently been saved and I have been helping her, via phone, to understand some of the things that are happening to her. She called me a couple of days ago, very frustrated. Her younger brother is going to be sent to Kuwait with his National Guard unit and is home with his wife and daughter for a visit before he leaves. He has two sons with another woman and doesn't want to see them. As a single mom she was quite upset with him, as she should be, but we had a conversation about what she could do about it. I got her calmed down, and then I started thinking about our Christian graces and how we are to handle them.

Colossians 4:6; "Let your conversation be always full of grace, seasoned with salt, so that you may know how to answer everyone."

Conversations don't always go the way we intended for them to go. They seem to take on a path of their own and go in a different direction than we thought. They can get heated to a point where we become angry and cause dissention and actually can push a relationship farther apart. Our conversations can be changed only by the grace of God. James in chapter 3 was very clear about this. As I told my granddaughter, you need to not let his attitude affect your relationship with him, pray for him to have a change of heart. Saying anything else will only make it worse and can cause you and him a lot of heartache in the future

Post note; At this time, several years later, he has a change of attitude and spends time with the boys.

This is what we, as Christians, should already know. She is just discovering God's outpouring of love and how to control what she says.

We, as seasoned Christians, should already be able to have control over what we say. Our speech and conversations should be seasoned with graciousness. The grace of God should be a way of life for us and it should affect how we communicate with others.

The second half of verse 6 says, *seasoned with salt.* Salt is used for preserving, cleansing and flavoring. This should be a reminder to us who have been entrusted with a new way of life to be an influence on people around us. Our conversations, when seasoned with God's grace, should and can be encouraging to others. It can show them the attitude of God. It can also preserve conversations from corruption. We must remember that our conversations with others need to reflect our life and our hearts. They should be transformed by God's grace.

Are we seasoned Christians, using our graces effectively or are we letting anger and the uncontrolled tongue keep us from using them to the glory of the kingdom?

Pray that your conversations and speech never lose its *saltiness.*

Have a great day and God bless!

Kay Ashwell

Love

Love God shows us

Good afternoon:

It's been several days since I sent out a thought. I guess my only excuse, which really doesn't matter, is that I have gone through a period of *what good does it do, it doesn't seem to make a difference.* That's a bad attitude for a Christian to have, and I ask God for his forgiveness.

He gave me a charge during this time of recovery and that was to watch over His sheep. I know we are all to do that, but this was a direct command from Him. I struggle to understand what that means and what I am to do, but He keeps encouraging me in different ways. One is to keep my granddaughter focused and on track, she is growing spiritually every day. Another is to send these thoughts out and so I try!

This week I had to praise God for the wonderful healing He is doing in my body. The doctor told me Wednesday that I made hip surgery look like a breeze and not the major surgery it is. The only one who gets credit for that is God and the peace and reassurance He gave me going into this surgery.

It also gave me the first hand knowledge of how much He cares for and loves me. With the love and care He has given me, how can I not follow His example as should each of us!

> 1 Corinthians 13: 6-7, "Love does not delight in evil but rejoices with the truth. It always protects, always trusts. Always hopes, always perseveres."

As Jesus faithfully bears our weaknesses, so we should faithfully bear His strength in helping others. As He believes our lives are worthy of his sacrifice for us, we should believe that proclaiming His good news of salvation is a worthy investment of our time. As He hopes we will willingly reflect His image, we should maintain the hope that whatever comes into our lives will show others His love, strength, and endurance.

As He endured the cross to provide us with eternal life, we should obediently endure this life with love and doing our very best for Him and to give to Him glory and praise.

He gave His life for us, we should give our best for Him. Whatever that entails and where ever that takes us, regardless of what we may want.

The following is an excerpt from a poem; 'The Love Within My Heart' by Shirley Hile Powell

I know not where to begin, my friend,
The love within my heart.
Now is the time to share,
Give them care and hope.
Help them find the strength to cope.
Everyday I try my best,
Let charity and love prevail,
Help others find their way.

If we give time to God and to each other, He will give us the time we need to accomplish our other tasks.

Have a great day and God bless you!

Love is pure

Good morning:

Another beautiful day and it is Valentine's Day, so first off, Happy Valentine's Day to each of you. What is Valentine day, and where did it come from? Valentine was the name of a Roman priest around 270 A.D. He was martyred by the Roman Emperor Claudius II. Valentine was caught marrying Christian couples and aiding other Christians who were being persecuted by Claudius II. At that time helping a Christian was against the law. He is known, in the Roman Catholic Church, as St. Valentine; since he married couples and gave his life for others, Feb.14 has become known as the Valentine or love day.

Love can be a confusing word in today's society. It is probably one of the most used, most misunderstood word in our language. Mixed messages are given for that word. Many of them can affect the way many look at love. For the child that is molested by their father and told it is because they love them, it can become something to fear. For a teen who is thrown out of the house and told it is because they are loved and they need to find out what life is all about, it can become something to hate. For most it is a word that brings with it, hurt, abuse, misunderstanding, and in some cases it is used in place of hate.

The world doesn't understand the true meaning of Love, only God can show us what true Love is.

> John 3:16, "For God so loved the world that He gave His one and only Son, that whoever believes in Him shall not perish but have eternal life."

> I John 3:16; "This is how we know what love is; Jesus Christ laid down His life for us. And we ought to lay down our lives for our brothers"

God's love is pure and is given freely to those who choose to follow His path for their lives. We need to stay close to him to be able to share His pure love to others.

> Galatians 2:20;"I have been crucified with Christ and I no longer live, but Christ lives in me. The life I live in the body, I live by faith in the Son of God, who loved me and gave Himself for me."

Paul, in his letter to the Corinthian Christians, gave us the true meaning of love in 1 Corinthians 13, also known as the love chapter.

> 1 Corinthians 13: 4-5, "Love is patient; love is kind; it does not envy; it does not boast; it is not proud; it is not rude; it is not self-seeking; it is not easily angered; it keeps no record of wrongs. Love does not delight in evil but rejoices with the truth. It always perfects, always trusts, always hopes, and always perseveres. "

This is who God is, He is pure love.

From the beginning God has shown His love and grace to His creation. His love cannot be matched. No one can love even themselves, until they know the love of the Father.

Love is what an abused child wants, it's what the teen that has been kicked out of their home wants, it's want the world wants, they just don't know how to get it. They therefore need to see the love that Christian's have.

Are you showing the world the kind of love that will lead them to Christ? If you are a true believer and you have Christ with you there is no excuse you can give that will justify you're not sharing that love with others. If you can't share it with others, Christians, non-Christians, the hurting, the injured, the sinners, you do not have the love of God in your heart.

You can pray all day, you can go to church every day, you can do good things and be a good person, but if you do not have the love of God in your heart, it means nothing. It takes two actions to have that love, First you have to accept it as a free gift from God, second you have to share it with others. If it doesn't have both actions it is not real. It cannot show the world what God wants for all His creation.

A prayer Paul prayed for the people in Ephesus, but it is one each of us needs to pray every day.

> Ephesians 3: 14-19; "For this reason I kneel before the Father, from whom His whole family in heaven and on earth derives its name. I pray that out of His glorious riches He may strengthen you with power through His Spirit in your inner being, so that Christ may dwell in your heart through faith. And I pray that you, being rooted and established in love, may have power together with all the saints, to grasp how wide and long and high and deep is the love of Christ, and to know this love that surpasses knowledge; that you may be filled to the measure of all the fullness of God."

As I leave you today, keep the love of God always in your heart, show it always to this sinful world and never let the evil one snatch it from you. Hold on to it and rejoice in it. Live it every day.

> Psalm 33:20-22, "We wait in hope for the Lord; He is our help and our shield. In Him our hearts rejoice, for we trust in His holy name. May your unfailing love rest upon us, O Lord, even as we put our hope in you!"

Keep that hope alive with the knowledge that the Father and the Son love you with pure love. The love of I Corinthians 13:4-8a.

Have a great day and God bless!

Love seen through us

Good morning:

When you travel do you go to different churches and worship? Do you ever notice the difference in how you are greeted or treated? Is there a difference between the larger churches and the smaller churches? If you haven't paid attention you should. There is usually a difference in how you are accepted. You may be greeted at the door of all of them, but how were you greeted? Was it a formal greeting of, we are glad you are with us today, handed a bulletin and left to find your own seat. Was it a greeting from someone who, while welcoming you, had a frown because you were not wearing the proper clothes? Was it a warm welcome with a smile and questions of where you were from, what you are doing in the area and introduced to others in the church? Did you feel welcome or just acknowledged?

A church who welcomes you with a warm smile, regardless of what you are wearing, makes you feel at home with them, and who are concerned about you, is a church practicing the love of Christ. James addresses this very thing in James.

> James 2:1-4, "My brothers, as believers in our glorious Lord Jesus Christ, don't show favoritism. Suppose a man comes into your meeting wearing a gold ring and fine clothes, and a poor man in shabby clothes also comes in. If you show special attention to the man wearing fine clothes and say, Here is a good seat for you, but say to the poor man, you stand there or sit on the floor by my feet, have you not discriminated among yourselves and become judges with evil thoughts?"

Jesus didn't discriminate, he healed the poor just as quickly as he healed the well to do. He taught everyone the same things, he ate with the outcast, the poor, and the wealthy. He welcomed everyone, took time to heal even the vilest of sinners. Wasn't afraid to touch a leper, or be seen talking to a prostitute. Jesus showed His love toward all people and without favoritism. This is what he expects us to do,

A few years ago there was a song or a movie about this very thing. I can't remember every detail, so forgive me if it is not exactly right. It was an older lady, I believe, who was expecting Jesus to come visit with her. She went out and spent her last dollars getting the things for a good meal to serve Him. She went home and prepared everything and waited. Pretty soon a hungry child came to her door and needed some food; all she had was what she had prepared for the Lord. But she gave the child a loaf of bread thinking the meal won't be ruined if there is no bread.

She waited some more and pretty soon a poor man came to her door cold and with no warm clothes. She thought if I build up the fire to warm this man I may not have enough wood for when the Lord comes; she thought I have blankets and I can set him close to this small fire and wrap him in warm blankets and he can take one with him. I will still be able to have a good fire for the Lord. So she brought the man in, sat him close to the fire and wrapped whim in blankets. After a time he warmed up and she gave him a blanket to wrap around him, some extra gloves and a warm hat, and he went on his way.

She waited some more and it was getting dark, soon she heard a knock and when she opened the door it was a traveler who was thirsty and needed a drink. She had only enough drink for the meal, but she couldn't let him go without giving him something to drink; so she gave him what she had. She would still have most of the meal for the Lord. He thanked her and went on his way.

She waited and waited and it grew late and she said Lord, I thought you were coming to visit me today? I came 3 times, I was the child you gave the bread to, I was the cold beggar who needed to get warm and you ask me in and warmed me and gave me warm things to wear, I was the thirsty traveler who needed a drink and you gave me what you had.

Matthew 25; 34-40; "Then the King will say to those on His right. Come, you who are blessed by my Father; take your inheritance, the kingdom prepared for you since the creation of the world. I was hungry, and you gave me something to eat. I was thirsty, and you gave me something to drink. I was a stranger and you invited me in. I needed clothes and you clothed me. I was sick and you looked after me. I was in prison and you came to visit me. Then the righteous will answer Him, Lord, when did we see you hungry and feed you, or thirsty and give you something to drink? When did we see a stranger and invite you in, or needing clothes and clothe you? When did we see you sick or in prison and go to visit you? The King will reply, I tell you the truth, whatever you did for one of the least of these brothers of mine, you did for me."

The time is at hand; the Lord will return soon, what are you doing for Him?

James 2:14-19; "what good is it, my brother, if a man claims to have faith but has no deeds? Can such faith save him? Suppose a brother or sister is without clothes and daily food. If one of you says to him, 'Go, I wish you well, keep warm and well fed', but does nothing about his physical needs, what good is it? In the same way, faith by itself, if it is not accompanied by action, is dead. But someone will say, you have faith, I have deeds. Show me your faith without deeds, and I will show you my faith by what I do. You believe that there is one God, Good! Even the demons believe that, and shudder."

What the world needs is to see the love of Christ coming from those who call themselves by His name. They don't want to just hear it; they need to see it in action. They need to be able to feel it. Each Christian and each Christian church needs to be reaching out and touching someone's life. It's not enough just to go to church and know what God says, it is necessary to put action into the knowledge. It is necessary to get off the pew and bring the love of Christ into someone else's life. It is time to stop thinking about what we need verses what others need. There are a lot of hungry, thirsty, hurting people who need to be shown God's love. If we don't do it who will? That is our responsibility, to put action into the faith and knowledge God has given us.

Today, show someone the love that you have been given, the grace and peace you have received. Don't hide it, use it. Put your faith to work with actions.

Have a great day and God bless!

New Year

New Year 1

Good morning:

As we come to the end of another year many things come to mind of what occurred in the past 12 months. There were problems to be solved, there was hurt that needed to be put to rest, there was frustration, along with the joy and good times with friends and family. To some it was a new way of life, a new path to walk, new responsibilities, and renewed hope.

Many will look back at the year remembering only the difficult, unfortunate things that happened in their life, they will have no joy. Others will look back at a year they were able to survive once again; to get by, to exist, but with no real hope for anything different in the New Year. Yet still some will look back at the year and be thankful for the opportunities they had this past year. Opportunities to serve God and follow His leading, they say good-bye to one year and look with expectation to the new year and the new opportunities it will hold.

Jeremiah was given this message for the nation on Israel 70 years into their captivity in Babylon. It still applies today, for many are captives in this sinful world.

> Jeremiah 29:11, "For I know the plans I have for you, declares the Lord, plans to prosper you and not to harm you, plans to give you hope and a future."

Yes, the Lord has plans for each of us. He knows what you have been through; he understands your concerns and worries. He will be with you, if you let Him. He has plans for each of us, plans of Hope. You don't have to be stuck in your present circumstances. Ask Him to show you the plans He has for you! God uses our situations to teach us to trust Him. He is faithful and will help us with whatever is in our life that needs fixing. Just ask Him.

God is hovering over you, teaching you how to fly, how to look forward to a new future.

> Deuteronomy 32:11, "Like an eagle that stirs up its' nest and hovers over its young, that spreads its' wings to catch them and carries them on its' pinions."

Have you ever watched an Eagle work with its young, to get them to fly? They hover over the nest, and then swoop down close to it so the updraft from its wings will help the young to lift out of the nest. It's there to catch it when it doesn't take flight and put it back into the nest. They keep this up until the fledgling spreads its wings and flies. Then they fly with their young teaching it along the way, how to search for food and sustain itself.

God is like that. He hovers over us, encouraging us, letting us decide when we are going to take that first step. Then when we do He is there to guide us, to pick us up and carry us on. He is always there, forgiving when we stumble, directing, teaching, and loving us as we struggle through life. But His guidance and teaching allow us to be able to soar, to be able to fly with Him, to grow and then be able to help others learn how to fly as well.

As we take those steps of faith to follow Him, He will bear us up on His wings of faithfulness and love. He will never leave us; He will always be there for us. He has plans for our future, plans so grand we can't imagine them; plans that give us *hope* of a better future; one with Him in paradise.

Is it time you took that step of faith and put your trust in Him and His plans for your life? Just reach out and ask and He will be there to guide you through the next year. A year that will bring many new and different situations; but ones He is there to help you through.

Have a great day and God bless!

New Year 2

Good morning:

As you begin to make those New Years resolutions, many that you won't keep, keep in mind that God's plan for your life is bigger and better than anything you can figure out on your own. You may have grand dreams of what you want to happen this year, but it is no match for what God has planned for you. His plans are infinitely higher than anything you could think of.

> I Corinthians 2:9, "However, as it is written, No eye has seen, no ear has heard, no mind has conceived what God has for those who love him."

> Romans 8:28, "And we know in all things God works for the good of those who love him, who have been called according to his purpose."

His purpose is for us is to love as He loves. As those resolutions are made remember to add respect to someone whose wisdom you utilized without proper acknowledgement. Add the debt of honor to someone who made things better this past year.

In the New Year we will meet challenges that could potentially divert us and even temporarily defeat God's purpose for our life. There may be failures to face, bad decisions or mistakes may be made, but if we give each day and each circumstance to God they will never defeat His plan for us. He can take those things, those situations and use them to accomplish His good and eternal purpose. God's plans can never be defeated.

What you dream may seem wonderful, but God wants to increase your wonder and joy by creating something extraordinary. God wants you to be so amazed at what he does that any memory of hardship fades away and you spontaneously praise Him.

Go ahead and make those resolutions, but the first thing on the list should be to put God in control of your life. When He is at the top of the list, and you trust Him to make the decisions for your future, nothing can happen that will defeat Him, not even the willful disobedience of people in the world.

When our purposes are aligned with His, even though God's will on our life is temporarily diverted by our mistakes, by circumstances, or by sin, we can never be completely defeated. Our responsibility is to keep cooperating with Him, to keep asking for His guidance, to keep following His command to love God and to love your neighbor. To do good to those who harm us and to give to others in the same way as we want them to give us, respect, love, honor, peace. Then God will always be there for us, to guide and direct us and to give us the hope and peace which was given on Christmas.

Have a great day and God bless!

New Year 3

Good morning:

As I sit here this morning my mind is going in many different directions all at once, so I hope my thoughts come together with some semblance of sense. We are less than 48 hours away from a new year. To many a new year brings with it the hope of a better life. You hear it all the time, it's a new year a time for new beginnings, a year that will be better than the last one, a year that I can get ahead in, a year my family will come together. Yes, we hear all sorts of things, all sorts of dreams, they spell *hope*. Hope for something better. But God being first in our lives is the only way we will achieve those dreams. He is the only one who can give us that hope.

There is a mythological Egyptian bird called the Phoenix, the story goes that it died in a fiery nest, only to emerge from the ashes as a brand new bird. That's what God wants to see in our lives. He wants us to emerge from the fires in our lives stronger, wiser, more loving, and more forgiving. He wants us to leave the negative things in our lives in the fire. He wants us to emerge a new person. Sometimes the fire in our lives is a spiritual one, when our inner being is being tested as if by fire. These are the ones we have to battle the hardest. This is the one we have to win and let a new person emerge after the testing, or during the testing, for then the fire can be put out. We can see our lives touch and inspire others by standing up for what we have gained.

As the year comes to a close I challenge each of you to make three lists; on the first one list the things you would like to see go away or that you want to give up; on the second list put the things you would like to see change in the new year, and on the third list are the things you are thankful for, the things you want to keep in your life.

When you have finished these lists I want you to thank God for the things and the people you listed on your third list. Next I want you to take the second list and ask God to help you achieve all the things you would like to see changed in your life. Take the first list, the things you want to go away and give everyone of them to God and ask Him to help you get rid of them. Then take that first list and burn it up, outside of course. As you watch it burn, remember that you have given those things to God and He will handle them from now on. Think on the positive things in your life and start to work on the things you want to see change with a new and positive attitude. Remember God is faithful to those who believe in Him. He will help you achieve them; you just need to keep asking for His help.

> Ephesians 1:15-21. In verses 17-19,"I keep asking that the God of our Lord Jesus Christ, the glorious father, may give you the spirit of wisdom and revelation, so that you may know Him better. I pray also that the eyes of your heart may be enlightened in order that you may know the hope to which He has called you, the riches of his glorious inheritance in the saints, and his incomparably great power for us who believe. That power is like the working of His mighty strength."

You have assurance of these things in God; He is going to help you achieve the desires of your heart; when you follow His instructions and follow in the ways He shows you. When you get discouraged and at your wits end, call on Him and He will see you through the tough spots. Commit everything to Him and know He will be there to help you through them.

> 2 Thessalonians 3:5, "May the Lord direct your hearts into God's love and Christ's perseverance."

Have a great day and God bless!

Kay Ashwell

New Year 4

Good morning:

The eve of a new year, what lies ahead for each of us? Only the Lord knows, but we will each play a part in how our year goes. It can be a positive year or we can let it be a negative year; it's our choice. If a positive year is what you want then you need to do whatever it is the Lord is asking you to do. That may be just to accept Him as your savior, it may be to start attending church regularly, or it may be He is asking you to serve in some capacity in your church, or it may be something bigger than you have the strength to do on your own. Whatever it is look to Him for help in doing it.

> Colossians 3:17; "whatever you do, whether in word or deed, do it all in the name of the Lord Jesus, giving thanks to God the Father through Him."

If you continue on in that chapter it gives you rules for a Christian household.

> Colossians 3: 19-21, "Wives, submit to your husbands, as is fitting in the Lord. Husbands love your wives and do not be harsh with them. Children, obey your parents in everything, for this pleases the Lord. Fathers, do not make your children bitter or they will become discouraged".

> Verse 23, "Whatever you do; work at it with all your heart, as working for the Lord, and not for men".

Read 2 Timothy 2:1-15 at some point today.

As the year comes to a close I am going to leave you with a *survival kit* for the year ahead. I can't give you these items in person but I can give them to you in words.

These are to remind us what we need to do!

- Pencil: to remind you to list your blessings every day.
- Toothpick: to remind you to pick out the good qualities in others and judge not.
- Band-aid: to remind you to heal hurt feelings, yours or someone else's.
- Rubber-band: to remind you to be flexible, things might not always go the way you want, but they works out.
- Tea Bag: to remind you to relax daily and meditate on your list of blessings.
- Mustard Seed: to remind you that your faith is stronger than you really think it is.
- Chewing Gum: to remind you that if you stick with it you can do all things.
- Candle: to remind you to share His light with others.

The following are promises the Lord has made to us!

- Comb: to remind you, that the hairs of your head He knows, therefore have no fear.
- Candy Bar: to remind you, that you will eat plenty and not suffer hunger.
- Nickel: to remind you, that He will supply all your needs.
- Eraser: to remind you, He forgave your sins and you must forgive others.
- Kleenex: to remind you that He will wipe away all the tears from your eyes.
- A Picture of Jesus Hugging you: to remind you that one day all of your trials and tribulations will cease and we will be together in peace.

Remember that *God loves you and wants the best for you*!

Have a great day and God bless!

Kay Ashwell

Obedience

Obedience in following God

Good afternoon:

Yesterday the lesson for my Sunday school class was about Abraham and his obedience to God when he was told to leave his home and go where God sent him Genesis 12:1-9. The story sounds like a simple task until you stop and analyze it. Abraham was asked to leave his home, his land, his country, and his people and blindly follow God's instructions. I asked the teens if they could have done the same thing. It would mean leaving their jobs, their homes, their family, and their friends and take only their car and go someplace they didn't know anything about.

Abraham had complete trust and faith in God. I wonder if we have the same trust and faith. Not only that, he had to love God to not be afraid to take that step of faith and trust.

> I John 4:18; "There is no fear in love, but perfect love drives out fear, because fear has to do with punishment. The one who fears is not made perfect in love."

So for Abraham and for us to do what God asks us to do we first have to have love for Him, love without fear. Then we have to have complete trust and faith in Him. I think most of us would say we love the Lord, but do we love Him with our very soul? What would we give up for God? Would we give up our home, our job, our family, our safety, our friends, and go where He directed us to go.

There are many, many places in scripture where we find this kind of love, trust and faith. In every one of them God is there to help them accomplish the things He had for them to do.

I believe Christians today have become impoverished in spirit. They want to hear, see, do and be where there are lots of things going on in the church. They want the church to tell them that life is fun, that all will be well if they just come to church and believe in God. They don't want to hear that they have to do anything or give up anything for Him. They don't want to have to kneel at the altar and ask forgiveness. After all, they come to church every Sunday, so why would they need to ask for forgiveness? They want God's blessings but they don't want Him to prune them or make them give up anything. I think the world and many Christians are living in a watered downed version of Christianity.

Christ came and suffered on the cross to make men good, not to make them feel good. Many Christians and the world have forgotten the suffering He went through for each of us. He still suffers when we don't respond to His calling the way we should. It grieves Him when we go on our own and don't rely on Him for guidance. When we think our way is the only way and we walk that path.

To be poor in spirit means to give up our pride; to mourn means to be penitent to the point of surrendering our sins; meekness means that we must surrender our very selves to the plans and purposes of God. Our hunger for God means turning away from our ambitions for all things: To be merciful means to pay good for the evil we have received. For purity we must give up all things impure. To make peace means to wholly choose God. These bring righteousness; they must be bought at a price. The price is total surrender of self to God. To be willing to go and do what He asks us, to forget about self.

To love, trust and have faith in our Lord means forgetting self and our desires and wants, to give Him total control. Are we there or are we *playing* at being a Christian?

Have a good day and God bless!

Obedience in standing firm

Good morning:

There is an old saying, *what a man sow's in life is what he will reap.* Another old saying is, *what a man thinks is what is in his heart.* What we think and do and say reveals what's in our heart. God is not fooled by our words, if our heart is not in the right place, He knows. Many men can give beautiful speeches, but if they don't believe what they are saying it is of no avail. Man likes to make things sound great so others will like them and think they are good, but many are only saying what they want others to hear, they are not speaking as one who believes what he is saying. It sounds good so they say it.

Jesus taught about the sown seed in Matthew 13, some fell along the road and were eaten by birds, some fell on rocky ground and sprouted quickly because the soil was moist but weathered when the sun came out, some fell among thorns where the weeds grew and chocked them out, and some fell on fertile soil and grew and produced much fruit. He goes on in that chapter and explains to the disciples what it means.

The seed which fell along the road is like anyone who hears the word of God and does not understand it; Satan comes and takes away what was sown in the heart. The seed which fell among the rocky ground is like the man who hears the word and accepts it with joy, but has no root so it lasts only a short time. When trouble or persecution comes, because of the world, he quickly falls away. The seed that fell among the thorns is like a man who hears the word but because of the worries of life and the deceitfulness of wanting wealth the word is choked out by the ways of the world. The seed that fell in good soil is like the man who hears the word and understands it. He will grow and go out and spread the seed to others.

In other words 3/4 of the seeds fell to the ways of the world. The other 1/4 are the ones who will receive the promises of God. Where are you in this? Are you one who hears but goes on and does what you want, not putting the word in your heart? Are you one who hears but isn't able to keep it, it is too hard so you just keep moving about in the world? Perhaps you are like the one who hears but can't give up the things of the world so you allow the world to hold you in its grip? Perhaps you are the one who grows and matures and is willing to stand up and be counted. The one who is strong and firm in their understanding of scripture?

We all have to decide who we are, what we stand for and how determined we are to meet Jesus in eternity. If you are one of 1/4 who allows the seed, which is the word, to rule your life then you will be the ones called by Him when the time comes. If you are in the 3/4's who have heard, and think that because you heard you will be called also. I'm sorry, but you won't be called, you will have to go through the tribulation and prove you are worthy to be with Him.

> Philippians 4:8, "Finally brothers, whatever is true, whatever is noble, whatever is right, whatever is pure, whatever is lovely, whatever is admirable - if anything is excellent or praiseworthy - think about such things."

Paul is saying to us what things people allow to occupy their minds will determine their actions and words. What we think should be on the things that God wants us to think about, and then to put into action what God wants us to do. This is the seed which fell on the good soil.

The time is short before we see our Lord come to take us home. Be diligent, be looking forward, and be about His business of spreading the word. Let your heart be pure and don't ever let Satan come in and take it away, not even for a minute. We have to be ready at all times to be called to Him. Be sure you are among the 1/4 that will make it. If you are not, you had better get that way real soon.

It is never too late to become hot for God.

Have a great day and God bless!

Persevere

Persevere in God's tasks

Good morning:

This past year I have had to face the fact that my body will no longer allow me to do the things I still want to do. It has come to the place where physically I can no longer be who I was a few years ago. But my imagination is still capable of many things. My mind has taken over what my body can't do any longer. My thoughts can do the things I can't do physically. When God is in control of your life He will give you whatever is needed to do the things He has for you to do. Even when our bodies can no longer be real active our minds can be, and God will use them in ways that will astound you.

> 1 Corinthians 2:9, "As it is written: No eye has seen, no ear has heard, no mind has conceived what God has prepared for those who love Him - but God has revealed it to us by His Spirit."

When we lose something, a job, our physical abilities, our health, God will call us to other things for Him. Sometimes losing those things are for our good so God can use us for what He needs. We may not understand it, it may even seem wrong to us, but we don't know what God has in mind for us to do. It may be something much greater.

It may seem like it is taking forever for God to show you what it is He is calling you to. Don't get discouraged, it may be when you feel like you cannot go on any longer that He will show you what it is you are to do. Scripture is filled with examples of men and women who, on the verge of disaster or failure, experienced God's creative work in their lives.

Remember:
God's Word is true.
God can part the sea.
God can heal the incurable.

God can provide water from a rock and manna from the sky in the wilderness. God can conquer your enemies.
God can still deliver from the fiery furnace and the lion's den.

God wants you to be amazed at what He does so that any memory of hardship fades away and you spontaneously praise Him. So if you are feeling like you have done as much as you can do, gone as far as you can go, remember God can take you farther than you ever dreamed you could go.

I may have mentioned a couple in their mid 50's who felt a call from God to ride a bicycle from the Pacific Ocean to the Atlantic Ocean in Florida.. He rode the bike, she followed in the car. They choose to do this because they felt God wanted them to bring awareness for the need of the children in South Africa, He would ride approximately 100 miles a day. They will finish their journey tomorrow. When a few of us, from our church, met them a few miles from here, they were about ½ way through their journey. God has given them the strength to complete this ride. He has kept them safe from harm. He has allowed them to witness to many along the way. They are humble people who praise God for every mile they have traveled giving Him all the praise and glory. They are quick to tell you they couldn't do it without God being with them every mile.

When God gives us a task to do, He is going to be there every mile along the way. He is going to give us the strength to accomplish it and keep us going. Even though my body is not as strong as it once was, my mind is sharp and God is using me to carry His word forward.

He still allows me to accomplish the things I need to get done. He allows me to use my mind a lot more; He has given me new insight into many things. And He has allowed me to have the strength to plant a garden. Took me four days to do what it used to take me only one to do, but it got done and now I can praise Him with each seed that produces, because He gave me the strength to do it.

Today, persevere in what He has asked you to do because your rewards will be more than you can think or imagine! David feels that way at accomplishing his cross-country ride; I feel that way as the beans, beets, and corn are peeping their heads out of the ground. It is to Him all praise and glory goes. It is to Him I give all the credit for being able to write every morning what He has given me to write. When God has been given control He can do things through you that you cannot even begin to imagine. It's all because He loves us so much He was willing to suffer and die for each one of us. Our lives take turns we can't explain, but He knows what He has for each of us, we just have to be willing to follow Him and be amazed.

Have a great day and God bless!

Persevere in lean time's

Good morning:

A beautiful day here in S.E. Texas; as I look out my window I see the leaves turning gold and red. It tells me fall is right around the comer. The air has the feel of fall. The moon seems brighter. Did you ever notice that in the spring and fall the moon seems to be brighter than in the summer and winter?

I am reminded:

> Ecclesiastes 3:1, "There is a time for everything, and a season for every activity under the heaven."

The trees and animals know the season is changing. They know it is a time to prepare for the harshness of winter. The squirrels are busy gathering in a storehouse of food; the plants are building strength to survive the winter. The trees are losing their leaves so the strength they have will carry them through the long months of winter.

Are we preparing for the new season in our lives? There are many things we will face in our life in the next few months. Things we know nothing about right now. The world is in a place in history that is causing us to consider where we are as Christians. Our faith will be tested in the months and years ahead. Are we prepared to face what it may bring?

We need to be storing up not only our daily needs of food and water; we need to be storing up the Word of God in our hearts. We need to be asking the Lord to fill our cup with Him so we can be wise, strong and able to face what lies ahead of us. We have no idea what the future holds, but He does. We have to depend on His promises.

The future for us is like the farmer who plants his crop in the spring and depends on the seasons, the rain and the sun to bring it to maturity

Kay Ashwell

and ready for harvest. God has given us a garden, our heart, to grow to maturity. He has given us our brain to be able to have the knowledge to know how to grow our garden. When we fill our brain with the right things it waters our garden, but when we neglect to put the necessary things into it, it withers and dies. Just like the crops the farmer plants, if it is not watered and cared for it will wither and die. His crop and our garden need to be watered with the right things to bring it to maturity. If you feel your life is like the dry ground of fall you need to ask God to give you the rain from heaven that will water your garden so you can become as strong as creation.

We see the seasons, the world, and our lives changing before us and we see that we need to be ready for these changes. The one thing that is constant and never changes is God's love for us. Scripture promises us that the Lord does not change.

Hebrews 13:8; "Jesus Christ is the same yesterday today and forever."

Look also at:

Hebrews 13: 5; "Keep your lives free from the love of money, and be content with what you have, because God has said, "never will I leave you; never will I forsake you."

He is the one constant we can depend on. The seasons change in their time, our lives change with each day, our country is in the grips of change, the world of tomorrow is in limbo. But we can be at peace because we have the Lord to help us face whatever will come. Our responsibility is to be active in the watering of our garden. For when He is there He will provide whatever is needed to keep it growing until harvest time. It is His desire that we experience the best in our lives. His love is always there, His strength is always there, and He will always be there when we ask Him.

Have a great day and may God bless you richly with His word!

Persevere through troubles

Good morning:

As Christians we have chosen a path that will get us to eternity with our Lord. But the path is not an easy one. Many people have the misconception that when they turn their life over to Jesus it will be an easy path, all their problems will go away and life will be a *bed of roses*. They soon discover that life is not easier, in fact it can get even more challenging, and they get discouraged and give up on the path. Or they continue to live as if there are no problems and never learn how to deal with them. They just keep moving from one place to another trying to find that *bed of roses*. They don't seem to realize those roses that smell so nice and look so beautiful, have thorns on them. The thorns of life which can prick us, tear into us, and leave scars on us.

God didn't promise us a life of luxury and everything we wanted, He did, however, promise us a life of peace and joy and forgiveness for our weaknesses. By putting our trust in Him we don't just magically have any more problems in our life; what we do have is God with us, helping us, showing us, giving us the things and the way to travel through life. Life is like climbing a mountain.

Some of you may have been in the mountains, and I don't mean the hills around here, I mean mountains. Mountains are beautiful to look at, they hold many wonderful treasures, but they also hold many dangers. There are beautiful valleys in them you can't even see unless you can get high up and look down. Also, they hold many wonders that you miss unless you are in the middle of them.

Our life with Christ can be the same as climbing a mountain. You start out on a path that is well marked and easy to follow. Things seem to go well for a time. Then you come to an obstacle in the path and you have to find your way around or over it. For some getting over it will take too much time, and will be a lot of work, so they often choose to get off the path and go around it. The problem is when you get off the path you may not get back on it. You can get lost real easy in the mountains because you are walking through a lot of brush and trees and have to make several turns in different directions to make your way through. If you don't have a clear view of the path it is easy to get lost and you get farther and farther away from the original path you were on. It is safer to clear the path of its obstacles, deal with them, and move on, even if it takes a little longer. You are still on the path and it once again gets easy to follow and just around that bend in the path you see a beautiful valley with running water and you can sit a bit and enjoy the refreshing water and rest. While the one who left the path to find an easier way around is still struggling with brush and other unseen obstacles that try to take him down. He hasn't found that resting place. He is still fighting all the obstacles he didn't know were there.

You can travel a long way on the path and not have any obstacles, but when they do show up, and they always will, you need to dig in, and clear the path of the junk and continue on the path which is visible. You may have many obstacles on the path, many times you may have to clear them out of the way, but the path is always before you. You can always see it and always know that it will lead you to the top where you will be able to marvel at God's goodness and mercy. You will find resting spots along the way and when the end is reached you can look back and know you have done the right things. You have stayed on the path through it all, even when you had to stop and clear the way.

The one who got off the path to find an easier way struggles all the way; they may eventually get to the top, but usually not in the same place that the original path led to. It may be on the opposite side of the mountain and even though they reach the top they don't know how to deal with all the frightening encounters they had from their trek. They sit there alone, trying to figure out how to deal with the fact that they don't know where they are and they don't know if they will ever find the place they set out to find. A few will eventually find the path and it will lead to the resting place, but many will stay lost, stay hurting, still struggling to reach the top, some will even be forgotten.

Yes, the mountains are beautiful, but when you start up that path you need to be prepared for whatever comes your way. You need the Savior with you, leading you, guiding you, helping you over the obstacles in the way, and always there to give you a hand. So when those obstacles show up and they will, hold firm to His hand, to His power, to His wisdom and let Him help you over each and every one of them. Don't get off the path and wander around lost in all the holes and bramble bushes that leave you with a lot of scars that have to heal, most often they will fester and become infected before they will close and heal over.

God has given us the path, He has given us the means to get over the obstacles, we just have to stay firm taking Him with us, each step of the way, not giving in to the thought that I can find an easier path if I follow my own ideas.

Have a great day and God bless!

Kay Ashwell

Persevere in a chosen path

Good morning:

This morning the word that keeps coming to mind is persevere, Webster defines that word as "to continue a course of action in spite of difficulty or opposition." This is a fitting description of our Lord. If anyone ever persevered it was Christ. He kept on doing what His Father asked Him to do under every condition man and Satan could throw at Him. He never gave in to the ways of the world. Under the cruelest of circumstances, He stood for what He believed in. Looking at His life should give us strength to persevere in our life. To stand for what we believe no matter the obstacles given us.

Too often in life we stand for a little while and then when things get real rough we turn and go a different direction, then ask God to bless us in our new journey. Isn't it wonderful that Jesus didn't do that on the way to the cross? He didn't want to go to the cross, what human would? It was a cruel, painful death. But He didn't go off the path he was given, He did what His Father wanted Him to do.

I'm sure the time in Gethsemane that night was one that we can't even fathom. A loving Father telling His only Son, I know you don't want to do this, but you have to in order to save our people from this sinful world. It says in scripture that Jesus sweat blood, I'm sure His decision was an agonizing one, but in the end He said your will be done.

> Luke 22:42, "Father, if you are willing take this cup from me; yet not my will but thine be done."

When things get tough in life do we persevere against all odds, do we stand firm in what the Lord is telling us to do, or do we stand for a little in the face of opposition and then take an easier way out using reasons that sound good to justify our actions?

Are there people in our lives who we have a conflict with, are there conflicts in our family, or with our neighbor? Do we approach our dealings with them negatively or positively? It is our responsibility to love them above ourselves. Not an easy task when we have been hurt or disappointed by them. It is easier not to be around them, but is that the path that God is leading you, or is He leading you to stand firm and stand up for what is positive and good in them and right for you? Paul was talking to the Corinthian Church when he told them in 1 Corinthians 9, that in order to win people to the gospel he became to them what they understood, keeping God's and Christ's law before him.

> 1 Corinthians 9: 22-23; "To the weak I became weak, to win the weak. I have become all things to all men so that by all possible means I might save some, I do all this for the sake of the gospel; that I may share in its blessings."

I'm not saying in order to save someone you have to do or be the way they are, but I am saying that sometimes it is harder on us and better for them if we persevere in the path and place God has called us to. Paul clarified his thoughts by saying he did it all while under the law of God and Christ which is to love God first, then to love our neighbor as we love ourselves.

The time is drawing short before His return, we have to be stronger than ever in our stand for God's kingdom. We are told in many places in Scripture to hold fast to our faith, to stand firm in our commitment, and to love those who are unlovable just as Christ loved us.

> Romans 13: 11–12, "And do this, understanding the present time. The hour has come for you to wake up from your slumber, because our salvation is nearer now than when we first believed. The night is nearly over; the day is almost here. So let us put aside the deeds of darkness and put on the armor of light."

> Verse 14 "rather, clothe your selves with the Lord Jesus Christ, and do not think about how to gratify the desires of the sinful nature."

Today expect the best, look for the positive things in others, show the love of God to each one you see. Smile at a stranger, say good-day to those you meet in your travels and persevere in your stand for our Lord.

Have a great day and god bless!

Persevere in life

Good morning:

There are days in each life when no matter what we do it seems to get us nowhere. It's like we are spinning our wheels for nothing. We just keep going, but for what? Paul in Philippians 3 is telling the Christians to forget what is behind them and to press on toward the goal before them.

> Philippians 3: 13 –14; "Brothers I do not consider myself yet to have taken hold of it. But one thing I do; forgetting what is behind and straining toward what is ahead, I press on toward the goal to win the prize for which God has called me heavenward in Christ Jesus."

To press on through the trials, the heartache, the confusion of life can be a daunting task in this world. I heard a story one time about a little boy who *stayed the course* and won a race. In Michigan each year, in the dead of winter, they have a kid's dog sled race on Lake Superior. This one year there were several teams of dogs and kids to race. This little guy was only 5 and only had one dog while the others had more dogs and were older. He was left behind at the start of the race, but about half way through the two leading sets of dogs got into a fight, as other teams got to them they joined in the fracas. When the little guy got to them he and his one dog went on past them and he was the only one to finish the race. He kept going, under all sorts of disadvantages. He had his mind set on finishing the race; he had his goal in mind. He knew where he was headed and nothing stopped him.

Life is that way. We can start out doing ok then we get to a spot where it seems we can't get past it and we get bogged down with all the little things that are in our way. We lose focus on what our goal is or where we are headed. We get all mixed up in the fracas of the world. We lose track of where we are going, sometimes we even go backwards for a time and have to go back over the ground we have already covered.

Kay Ashwell

It's hard to press forward when things are stacking up against our progress, our load keeps getting heavier and heavier, but God has called us to a purpose and He will never leave us hanging there in turmoil when it is the goal we are striving to reach. We need to keep that goal in front of us at all times. God will help us reach the goal as we press forward to win the race here on earth. A race which we have to keep winning and pressing ever onward to reach, the goal set before us, eternity with Him.

Paul never gave in to the sufferings of life when it would have been easy for him to return to his former comfortable life, the little boy never gave up the race even when the odds were stacked against him, Jesus never gave up the task set before Him, the Cross. We can't give in to the pressures of life and the world trying to pull us down, we have to stay the course, we have to finish the race; we have to press ever onward toward the goal set before us, eternity with Him.

> Joshua 1:9, "Have I not commanded you? Be strong and courageous. Do not be terrified; do not be discouraged, for the Lord your God will be with you wherever you go."

Have a great day and God Bless!

Persevere in our Christian walk

Good morning:

There are times in our lives when it seems as if nothing is going in the right direction and everything is in turmoil and turned upside down. Some of the time things go smoothly and sometimes things are just pieces all scattered about. Those are the times when we have to let God help us put things together, to fit them into place.

It's like putting a jigsaw puzzle together. We start out putting the corners and the edges together to form the base of the picture; the straight edges, the things that hold everything in place. The rest of the pieces are all mixed up and we have to start sorting them out and finding the ones that go together. Sometimes we can find pieces that fit into the edges making them bigger and wider and stronger. Sometimes something in the middle catches our eye and we start working on it and then we are working from the inside out. Putting a large puzzle together can take weeks. It may take many days to put it together depending on how much time you work on it. Some get tired of working on it and just give up and it sits for days until they get the desire to work on it again. Sometimes the puzzle never gets done, it is just left sitting there undone or it is put up and out of sight never to get finished.

Our walk with the Lord is much the same. We start out putting our walk with Him together with a strong desire, making a strong foundation to stand on. Then the things of life and the things of this world start to invade our space. Things aren't fitting together as they did at first. Trials and confusion start to take over. We can't see the whole picture any longer. Sometimes the harder we try to fit the things together they just won't go. We get frustrated; sometimes we get hurt while we are searching for something that fits together. Sometimes we see something that looks good and we start to build on it only to find that it doesn't go anywhere. It just sits there, undone, until we find the things that go with it so it can be attached to the strong foundation we had to start with.

Kay Ashwell

Each piece of our life has to fit into the next piece to keep the picture coming together. The picture of our life takes time to connect all the pieces together. Sometimes if we get discouraged and disappointed in life, we can't find anything to help it grow. We just sit and worry and stew and fret and go nowhere. If we don't pick things up and start putting them together again it will never come together.

In order for us to complete the picture of our life we have to keep working on it. With God's help each day we can find the pieces that are supposed to fit together. It takes time and effort and guidance from Him, but as we learn to follow Him He shows how each piece fits together. Until we have it completed.

The key to putting a puzzle together is the joy and fun and pleasure it gives us to finally find the pieces that fit and then finally see the complete picture. We need to have fun putting the pieces of our life together. We should be able to see joy as each piece fits into the next. We are growing, maturing, becoming the person God intended for us. Yes, there are setbacks, discouraging times, times when we would just like to give up, but we can't if we want our life complete, one we can have fun with and enjoy along the way. That's when we can see God working in and through us so others can see Him too.

Our joy and peace comes from God as each step we take leads us closer to the life He intends for us, The life that will be complete when He returns and takes us home to be with Him. The more pieces that are put together through His strength and guidance the closer we come to that time when we will be complete. Stand firm in Him and keep building that picture of your life. Call on Him when things get out of order and let Him help you get it working again.

He is the strong foundation of life; the one who can help put the pieces all together. The one who keeps us moving forward and not giving up.When you feel like giving up just go to Him and ask and He will help you find that next piece that fits into the picture of your life.

Have a great day and God bless!

Peace

Peace in life choices

Good morning:

There is a saying which I have heard since I was a young girl, and that was a long time ago. It says, *God moves in mysterious ways, His wonders to perform.* As I look back on my life of 70+ years, I can see where God was been at work in it many, many times.

Although I don't readily remember some of the times He was there, other times stand out vividly in my mind. It's easy to recognize the big things in life when you know He was the one who took care of you, because no one else could have. It's all the little things He does that most don't recognize as Him at work in their life. I can remember as if it were yesterday several times when He spoke or acted directly to change my life. I have to sit quietly and be reminded of other times when He was there, directing me, guiding my every footstep, and during some of these quiet times I can see where He was carrying me along in this life. Times when I was too hurt, too grieved, too self motivated, too angry, to let His knowledge get through. These are times we don't realize until they are long gone and we look back and say, why didn't I do that or see that at the time?

We can all relate to these moments in our life. But the *what if moments* are gone, never to be lived again, at least I hope they won't be lived again. When we see in hindsight we can see clearly all the times and things He has done for us during our life. Only in hindsight can we recognize the agony we must have caused, not only to our earthly family, but also our heavenly family. I can almost hear Him, when He says, *not again child, I thought we got through this one already.*

Some of those times we thought, *man was I lucky,* or you look at something with the eyes full of pride you think *look what I have done on my own.* When we reflect on our life, which we all need to do, it's in those times when we can see how God had a hand in what we accomplished and in what we were able to do. Other times when we reflect on our life we can see where the right people were always there at the right time to help give us the strength and ability to carry on. As we look back over those times we ask ourselves, how was I able to get through that, how did I manage to accomplish that. That's when we realize we didn't, God did. Yes, in looking at hindsight it's easy to see how God has worked in our lives.

So why don't we get smart? Why don't we learn? Why do we have to reflect on things before we know why they happened? The simple answer is, because we are human. But, we can learn through them how much we depend on God without even actively trying.

The hardest atheist, the one who refuses to recognize God, the one who shuns God all their life never acknowledging Him for who He is, will at some point before they die, have to face the fact that God had a hand in saving them from some disaster, some horrible fate. It's at that time they have to make a choice to accept Him as the one who saved them, who protected them, or to ignore Him. They have to either recognize Him and turn from their unbelief, or keep ignoring Him and lose eternity.

God is always trying to bring the unsaved to Him, He desires that all be saved, but He knows that will never happen, many will never recognize His love, or will choose to keep doing and thinking as they always have. The choice is always ours to make. We can choose the right way and face our mistakes, accept our weaknesses, own up to our sins, and ask Him to lead and direct us, or we can choose to keep doing and thinking the way we always have, ignoring Him and His part in our life. He will never force us. He never told us life would be easy, He will never tell us life is a *bed of roses*. But He did promise that He will walk with us, carry us, and give us wisdom and understanding to get through this life.

It is our choice, to accept Him or deny Him. As for me, I choose, and have chosen for most of my life, to follow Him. Not that I have done everything right, not that I haven't sinned, not that I haven't made Him unhappy, but I have always loved Him, always recognized Him in my life. I always came back to Him. He is my strength; He is where my heart is. I know I can count on Him to give me the strength to face whatever this world throws at me. He is always with me; I can always feel His presence in my life. I can give to Him all my worries, all my concerns, all my frustration, all my anger and He will take them and use them to grow me, to mature me, to teach me new things, to give me more wisdom, more understanding. He is what nurtures me; He is the one who gives me peace. He is the one who keeps me on the right path.

He can give you this same peace, this same assurance, this same hope, you just have to make the right choice and accept Him. You have to ask Him to help you, to give everything over to Him.

> John 14:23-24, "If anyone loves me, he will obey my teaching. My Father will love him, and we will come to him and make our home with him. He who does not love me will not obey my teaching. These words you hear are not my own; they belong to the Father who sent me."

Yes, we have a choice. I pray your choice is the same as mine has been for most of my years on earth. My mother is almost 93 and has, and still does, know who has kept her all these years. She gave me that knowledge as a child, and now we can share, in our older years, all the wonderful things He has done for us. We can give Him glory and praise for keeping us safe, healthy, and on the right path. It is never too late to find the right path. Just ask for it. He will show you. Then let Him help you follow it.

Have a great day and God bless!

Note to Reader: My mother was called to her heavenly home in May 2018 at the age of 99 1/2 years.

Peace in help for others

Good morning:

It is the beginning of a long weekend, many will be traveling and visiting family, and many will be in a hurry and will forget their responsibility to each other. It is a weekend where many only think about what they are going to get to do and they won't care about what anyone else wants or needs. It is a time when people will be in such a rush they will forget the laws and many will be hurt or killed because of the careless acts of others. There have been many disasters in our country this spring. Many of our countrymen are still not back into normal situations. Many are still displaced in recovery centers, many will not be able to enjoy the holiday with a friend or family member because they are stranded in flood waters or they have lost everything and can't get to family.

The Christian who really cares for his fellow man will be about the business of helping others who are lost and alone. Yesterday, I was shopping and the store and parking lot were overcrowded. I have had trouble with my back since my hip surgery. In fact my back was giving me trouble before my surgery. We have handicap stickers on the car because of Don's breathing problem and when I got done at the store and was back out to the car, I was hurting pretty good. This lady was headed into the store, I suspect, to get what she needed also, but she stopped and asked if she couldn't help me unload my basket into the car. She took the time to make sure someone else received the help they needed. She was willing to stop and assist even though it was about 100 degrees out. As Christians we should be doing the same all the time. I was hurting, but not like some others are hurting, it only takes a few minutes to stop and help someone who may need a hand. You never know but what that person may need a smile, a reassurance that the world has not forgotten them. They need to know that someone cares.

Don and I often go to the senior center for lunch. There is this man who comes in quite often and always sits in the same seat, does the same thing every day and leaves as soon as he is finished eating. He happens to sit in a seat close to where Don and I sit and I always ask him how he is doing. His answer is always the same, I'm here, aren't I? I smile and say to him I'm glad you could get here today. You have a great day.

Well, the other day Don was sleeping because he had worked all night, so I went by myself. I was a little early and I was sitting at the table when he came in. He always walks behind me and goes and gets a bag of popcorn and then comes back on the other side of the table. When he went by he tapped me on the shoulder in greeting; and when he came back I was looking out into space and didn't see him coming. He stopped in front of me and said, where is that smile today, having a problem? I assured him I was fine and smiled at him and when he sat down he turned to me and asked where Don was. He even entered into a short conversation with another lady and me. Now that may not seem like much to you, but it showed me that even though this man had never entered into any conversation with anyone this past year, he noticed when I didn't greet him and smile at him. He missed it and had to make sure everything was ok. His separating himself from everyone else was easing; he was allowing others to communicate with him and he was communicating with others.

Simple acts of kindness, friendliness, and caring make a difference in someone else's life. It doesn't take much from us, but it may mean a whole lot to someone else. These are all opportunities to be God's witnesses here on earth. To you it may be just a smile; to someone else it may be the only smile they get all day. It may be the only good thing to happen to them. Smiles and greetings cost us nothing, but they may be the most important gift that another may receive.

Jesus shared Himself with whoever needed Him. He stopped and helped those in need and He showed us how we are to do the same. Jesus went the extra mile for others; He went to the cross for each of us.

It takes little time to assist someone else; it takes no time to smile at someone. We need to stand out in this world, not become just another body in a sea of bodies. People need to see the difference in us; they need to feel the kindness, the joy, and the fellowship of others.

So this weekend whatever you are doing, where ever you are going, take Jesus along with you, not just for you but for someone else also. For a stranger who you may meet. For that someone who may need a lift in their day. It won't slow you down and it won't hurt you in any way, but it may help someone else forever.

Let Jesus shine from you in everything you do and say. Be a good witness, not a so, so witness for Him.

God bless you, have a great weekend!

Peace in turmoil

Good morning:

I'm late again this morning, not because I was sleeping, but because I am being tested today. But God is bigger than Satan and He will take control. I guess because of things here my thoughts are going in the direction of peace. Webster has several meanings for peace, but the one I am looking for is serenity, calm, and quiet. This is the peace that God gives us when we call on Him to assist us through the testing and trials of life.

There is one requirement to attaining that peace and that is that we have to be reconciled to Him. Reconcile means to make right, we have to make things in our life right with God. We need to be in accord with Him. He accepts us where we are, but we have to be sincere in our walk with Him. We can't ride the fence; we can't be on again off again and expect Him to give us the peace we want. We have to stand steady in our walk with Him. We have to do the things He has asked us to do and be the person He expects us to be.

We have to give up the things that are not of Him, our desires and wants have to be turned over to Him. Our anger, frustrations, our lying, our cheating, all have to be given over to Him and then not taken up again. We have to be at peace with our family and friends and we have to be in fellowship with other Christians so we can remain strong. Satan likes to keep us away from church for one reason or another to weaken us so we fall back into our old ways and fall back into sin.

Temptations come every day; we have to have the strength to walk away from them. Temptations are not sin unless we give in to them. We need to stay in tune with God to be able to not give in to temptations. We have to keep the communication open with the Lord to keep His peace in our lives.

2 Corinthians 5 tells us how to be reconciled to God. We are His offspring and we are to take the message of reconciliation to others so they may have the peace that we have by being His child. The world is seeking peace; they don't know how to get it. We do, God gives us His peace and shows us the way..The world will not receive His peace until it recognizes that He has dominion over everything. He created everything in and on the earth. He has given us Jesus so we can be reconciled to Him and know his love and peace in our lives.

> Psalm 29: 10-11, "The Lord sits enthroned over the flood; the Lord is enthroned as King forever. The Lord gives strength to His people; the Lord blesses His people with peace."

God gives you perfect, unfaltering peace through the protective power of the Holy Spirit. Understand that through the trials, temptations, and conflicts in life the one who is perfect is working to bring peace to His children. Depend on it, relax in it, and pass it on to others as it is our responsibility to do.

God bless and have a great day!

Peace through Christ

Good morning:

Turn to Romans 5:1-8 this morning. In it you will read the love, the peace, the joy, and the hope that we have in Christ Jesus.

Many people in the nation today will be claiming that Obama has given the nation new hope. When in fact what he gave the nation was a pretty speech. The things he says we need to address are facts that we face, positions we have put ourselves into by not standing up and being counted as Christians for this nation in the past 30 years. The place we are in as a nation has come over many years and won't go away just because someone gives a good speech.

Romans 5 gives us the answer, are we as a nation ready to hear what He has to tell us or are we going to continue to go about beating each other up if we don't agree with each other's views? It matters not to God if you are a democrat, a republican, an Independent, or any other political group. What God is interested in is, are you a true believer, will you be strong as a Christian and follow His leading? Will you stand up and be counted as His? He cares where your *heart* is.

Peace with God is not just a feeling of peace of mind, but rather a new relationship with God. Once we were His enemies, but now we are His friends, part of His family. We have been given direct access to God.

The heavy curtain that separated us from God in the past has been removed and we can come before God and have a personal relationship with Him. We will go through sufferings of one sort or another but we should praise Him for them because they produce perseverance, perseverance builds character and character shows hope. Hope is not something someone else can give us; it is not built on unfounded optimism, but on the blessed assurance of our future destiny and is based on God's love for His creation, man. It is given through the Holy Spirit and demonstrated to us in the death of Christ.

We see the love of God and the hope for humankind being given to us when we were sinners, when we followed after the things of the world. When we were powerless to do anything about them or even acknowledge them. Christ died for all mankind, for all the ungodly of the world. Do we then accept this love, this joy, this hope or do we trample it in the ground because we can't or won't allow God to be the center of everything we do?

This nation was once great, because its leaders were God loving, God fearing men. They were not afraid to stand up and say this nation was founded on the principles of God. In order to maintain, as a great nation, we need to once again have men and women as our leaders who believe in God. Anyone can stand and give a pretty speech, but unless they are letting God direct them they are only words. They will do nothing.

> Romans 5: 8; "But God demonstrates his own love for us
> in this: While we were still sinners, Christ died for us."

How long are we going to keep Him on the cross? How long before this nation goes to their knees and begs for God to return to us?

As Christians we have a responsibility to show the nation how to change things. We have a responsibility to God to be the light through which He can shine once again. Pray that the Christians in this country come together as one and become strong and stand up for God.

Pray for those in the Senate and in the House who are Christians to become bold and stand firm, believing, so the nation can see what it needs to do. Pray for each other that as brothers and sisters in Christ we become the Church that God is looking for. One that follows His path and that we stop devouring each other. When these things begin to happen, a revival in this nation will take place.

God wants a holy people, not people who are weak and change like the direction of the wind from day to day. Decide for yourself if you are going to be strong or continue to be a weak Christian. Are you still drinking milk as a baby or are you able to chew meat as a mature person? As for me, like Paul, I am reaching ever forward to the future I will have with my Lord.

Have a great day and God bless!

Prayer

Pray to be a good disciple

Good morning:

First today I must ask your forgiveness, I have not been very faithful in bringing you positive thoughts the last couple of weeks. I could use all sorts of excuses, but the fact is I have been searching for answers and direction and it has been fruitless. Sunday pastor was using John 15, the vine and the branches. What struck me was not what he was saying, but what God said to me.

> John 15: 8; "This is to my Fathers glory, that you bear much fruit, showing yourselves to be my disciples."

That passage in John 15 tells me that I must be a disciple, and that's how I am to watch over His sheep.

So what does being a disciple mean? The definition in scripture is, having a serious personal relationship with Jesus. It means we are all to be His disciples.

> John 14:12–14; I tell you the truth, anyone who has faith in me will do what I have been doing. He will do even greater things than these, because I am going to the Father. And I will do whatever you ask in my name, so that the Son may bring glory to the Father. You may ask for anything in my name, and I will do it."

I ask myself how can I do greater things than He did. It is not talking about bigger miracles, it is about honoring God. Jesus' purpose was to provide the way to God so that others could know Him. Our purpose is to be His representatives, to bring to others a visual image of Christ so they can and will come to know Him as we know Him.

How do we do that? Prayer is the key to making us productive disciples for the kingdom. We need to pray to soften and enlighten our entrenched values, perspectives and priorities. We are to be holy as He is holy and walk as Jesus walked. By this others will see Him in us. We must encourage, adopt and help others walk as He walked. God intends for His disciples to absorb the passions, dreams, and secrets of the master. Jesus showed us how to be disciples by His very presence on this earth. He walked in love, spoke in love, and went to His Father for direction and strength. That's what we must do, walk in love, speak in love, and pray for direction in our lives and for what His will is for us.

Each of us may be led down a different path to accomplish His will, but as long as we are faithful to the direction He is leading us, we can be sure of one thing; He will be with us all the way. We all have different abilities, different talents and we are to let Him direct that path, but we are all part of His family, and we are all to be disciples in the area that He has called us. When we know whose we are and when we are walking with Him, we will be available to be the disciple He can work through to bring others to Himself. This is how we can all watch over His sheep!

Have a great day and God bless everything you do for Him!

Pray for a full cup

Good afternoon:

This A.M. started out hectic and a trip to town was on the agenda to see the doctor. My quiet time has been the last couple of hours, and it made me stop and reflect on my last thought. As I walked around Wal-Mart getting the few things I needed I ran into several Christians which made my morning a pleasant one. It also had me seeing many wandering around with McDonalds coffee cups in their carts.

I thought isn't that what many see the morning for? They wouldn't think of starting their day without at least one cup of coffee. They need that first cup to wake them up and get them going into their day. Don't get me wrong I like a good cup of coffee too.

Then there are those who see the morning as a time to begin their day with prayer, a song and perhaps bringing a moment of joy and peace to others. This is a time to reflect on how gracious our Lord is. How faithful He is in taking care of us. How peaceful our day will be because we have chosen to begin our day with Him.

For us who praise Him for all His blessings, our day is not without conflict, rushing, or frustration, the difference is we have given the day to Him and He will help us through each and every one of the obstacles we encounter. Our hearts are at peace and we can handle each situation with His help because He is ever with us. What a blessed peace that is. To rest in the Lord all day regardless of what it has to throw our way.

How difficult each day must be for those who don't know Him or who start their day without giving it to Him.

A popular song sung by Jessy Dixon, Fill my cup, Lord; I lift it up, Lord. Come and quench this thirsting of my soul.

It is important to start the day with our Lord, to have Him fill our cup so we can survive in this world we live in today. How sad for those who don't wake up with a cup of quenching, clear water from Him. How sad they have to try to start and go through the day with a cup of coffee. Not that there is anything wrong with coffee. But for us the Morning Prayer is a time to have our cup filled to overflowing with peace. That allows us to connect with others and give to them that same peace. The good news is, we have an unlimited number of refills that are readily available any time we feel our cup becoming empty throughout the day. I wonder how those who depend on coffee to start their day can actually cope with their day.

Thanks and praises to our Lord for giving us the opportunity to be filled with Him each morning.

I pray each of you are taking that opportunity and privilege.

Have a great day and God bless you richly!

Pray for guidance

Good afternoon:

This has been a rather busy, exasperating week for Don and me. As I sit here looking out my window at all the trees and the Rose of Sharon bush in my back yard, I know the difficulties we had this week will all be worth it. I am sorry I have not been in touch this week but I have been so exhausted my mind has not been too focused. We did manage to get us and our R.V. on our property.

God has the power to accomplish anything He wishes. He gives us that same power if we would only use it. So why is it we go about trying to do some of these things on our own?

> Psalms 68:35; "You are awesome, O God, in your sanctuary; the God of Israel gives power and strength to His people, Praise be to God!"

I found myself saying several times this week, praise God, and thank you Lord. As I reflect back, however, I am wondering why I didn't ask for His help when things were a little hectic instead of waiting until it was over to say thank you. He would have been able to direct our process from the beginning. I think we all fail to call on Him first and when things get a little rough we call on Him to help us out.

> Proverbs 4:11-12, "I guide you in the way of wisdom and lead you along straight paths. When you walk, your steps will not be hampered: when you run, you will not stumble."

Even though we know these things we, in a moment of confusion, trouble, or problems, forget to ask for that guidance. God's will is for us to be so close to Him that we are confident He is always leading us. God knows the way, the best way, for us to go.

Years ago I read a book about being in constant prayer with the Lord, I strive to do that, but alas, there are times I forget and then I struggle. Paul said, pray without ceasing, I can do that a lot of the time, it took years of practice, but there are those times that are so hectic, so rushed, so pushed for time, that we just go ahead with the first thing that comes into our heads. It's good to reflect and remember that God knows the best way for us to go.

> Isaiah 30:21; "Whether you turn to the right or to the left, your ears will hear a voice behind you, saying this is the way; walk in it."

You and I need to continually seek His will in everything we do. It may not seem like the easiest way, or the right way, but God knows what is best for each of us and will work in us to perfect us. The road may be bumpy and narrow and hard to follow, but when we reach the end of that road the way will be clear and we will know why we had to go in the direction we did.

So as I once again struggle to pray unceasingly I praise God for the path He has lead me on, struggles and all, rough road and bumpy, through darkness and shadow, for I know He leads me to the purpose for which He has planned for me.

God bless and have a great afternoon and a great tomorrow!

Pray to focus on time

Good morning;

It's Wednesday, hump day, as we called it when I was a girl. The middle of the week meant we were half way to another weekend. Days seemed long back then, except for Saturday and Sunday. They seemed to fly by. The weekend was over, just to start a new week. Then there was summer and after about a month everyone was ready to go back to school to see friends and find out how everyone else was and what they did. When we did get back and talked to them, we got jealous of some for the things they did. Things we didn't or couldn't do. For some of us we had to work all summer and didn't get to go anywhere and we were glad it was time to go back to being a student.

It's almost the end of July and there are many who will be returning to school in the next two to three weeks. The school supplies are out, the stores are pushing fall clothes and parents are anticipating the time when school will start again. For some summer has been short and has gone by too fast. The older I get the faster the days seem to go. One flows into the next and before you know it another month has gone by and I have no idea where it has gone.

As Christians our days can go like that. We get lazy with our prayers, we let worries sneak in and cause us to falter in our daily walk with God. We let the troubles of the times control our minds, doing things that take over our time and we don't give God the time to keep us from folly. The things of this world that offer us temporary pleasure or that boost our egos seem to take over. When we put these things in front of spending time with God, or doing the tasks He has given us; we are putting ourselves in danger of fashioning idols out of things that shouldn't be. We sometimes take God out of the number one spot in our life. When other things are taking His place in our life, it's then that our lives become darkened and we become discouraged, disappointed, and even angry that we can't do or have the things we think we want and need.

King David gives a thought to bring us back into focus of where we should be.

> Psalm 86:11-13 "Teach me your way, O Lord, and I will walk in your truth; give me an undivided heart, that I may fear your name. I will praise you, O Lord my God, with all my heart; I will glorify your name forever. For great is your love, toward me; you have delivered me from the depths of the grave."

We need to refocus our lives, refocus our priorities, and refocus our prayers. We have to stand up and be counted for God if we expect Him to bless us. We have to get back to our roots, back to giving God the control and back to praying. Prayer can and will be the only thing that will change our lives.

Have a great day and God bless!

Pray for God's blessing

Good morning:

It is so easy to get caught up in the things of the world, to let them become more important than God is in our lives. We all do it and it is time to get back to letting God be in control. We wonder why things don't go as they should, why we are having a hard time, why life is so hectic and frustrating and we don't stop to ask God to show us His ways. We just keep going, doing what we have been doing and say bless me Lord.

What have we done for Him? Why should He bless us? We have let other things take control and have put Him on the back burner or our lives and of our country and then expect Him to bless us. People are seeing what apathy does when no one steps in to stop it. The Christians of this nation have been apathetic far too long. They have just sat back and said it will get better; God is the one in charge. Well yes, God is in control, but He will let Satan have his way when God's people don't do anything to stop it.

This nation has turned its back on God; the Christians have allowed it to happen by not standing up and saying no. They have let it happen by not praying for God's will. They have just voted because someone was liked, or popular, not for what the person stood for. What his or her beliefs were. We didn't take the time to find out. We just went in and voted, usually down party lines. Did we do it after we had prayed asking God to show us who to put in office or did we just go vote because it was what we were supposed to do? Or did we not vote because we were too busy to stop what we were doing or if voting day interfered with what we wanted to do? This nation is in the fix it is in because we, the so called Christians, let it happen.

We need to come together in prayer, we need to take a stand and be heard. We need to get out of our apathetic state and become the men and women God has called us to be. We can't just sit and do nothing and expect God to do it all. He called us to do His work, to be His witnesses, to stand up for what is right and to put what is evil out of this world. We need to be praying for God to intercede. There is an old saying, *a house divided against itself can't stand*. Well, a heart divided between God and the world cannot be where it should be. A country divided cannot stand.

My prayer is to heal our land, bless our land with honorable industry, sound learning, and pure manners, keep us from violence, discord, confusion, pride, and every evil way. Protect our liberties, and help us to become one united people. Grant the spirit of wisdom to those we have chosen. To God we entrust the authority of government. We trust that there may be justice and peace at home,, through obedience to your law, we may show praise for you among the nations of the earth.

My prayer to help us: Lord, give me the strength and wisdom and courage to stand up for you. Give me the strength to keep you first in my life so I am an example to others. Give me the courage to defend you in the face of conflict. Give me peace to know that you are with me and will be with me through it all.

God bless!

Pray for God's will

Good morning:

Do you realize when you pray you are expressing love for God as well as for your neighbor or a stranger? Prayer is powerful, when your prayers are sincere, and caring. They should not be so automatic that you do not even think about them. Jesus prayed a lot for His Fathers will to be done. He went often to His Father with His concerns.

Paul learned that prayer was the key to being able to carry out God's plans and His work. He prayed and praised God even when He was in prison for the privilege of serving Him. Are our prayers as sincere? Or do we just do them because we are supposed to? Do we really pray that God will intervene on behalf of someone or something or do we just make motions that we care and are cold to the situation? Do we really mean what we pray?

The Christians in this nation should be joining in an earnest prayer asking God to bring this nation back to Him. We should be praying that God's will be done here on earth. We should be praying for each other. It bothers me, and I guess it even stifles my prayers, when I am asked to pray for someone or something and then told I can't share that with anyone. It seems to me if someone or something needs to be prayed for there shouldn't be a limit on who can pray for it. I can't find anywhere in scripture where it says only certain people should be praying.

I can find, however, many places where it says to pray in God's name, to pray always, to pray for your neighbors, to pray for the saints, to pray for the unsaved, to pray for our enemies, to pray for God's will in all things. If someone doesn't want details shared all they have to do is ask for an unspoken request. But if it is important enough to ask for prayer, I don't get this idea of limiting who can pray. It's the same as saying I want you to pray but I don't trust just anyone to pray. It seems a little selfish to me to want prayer, but only certain people can pray for it. God already knows what needs to be done; He just wants others to lift the needs up, to share with one another in love and support.

For me, if I have a great need, or I have a family member or a friend or a fellow Christian who needs prayer I want as many as can to be praying. I believe He knows the heart of everyone who lifts a prayer up for someone else. When we are praying for someone else we are asking Him for His protection on them and on the situation. I do not believe that He won't answer prayer if one person is not praying in the right sprit. Let as many prayers as can, be lifted up. He hears the prayers of those who are sending them up in love and deep concern for the situation or the person, whose hearts are in the right place. It is not our place to decide who should and who shouldn't pray.

Sometimes when you pray you don't even know who you are praying for. But if your heart is right, if you are praying in earnest that God will intercede in whatever situation arises He will hear your prayer. Prayers are like sweet love songs to God, He loves to hear them, even if they are not perfect. Sometimes I get the feeling that I should just pray and I don't know why or for what. I just ask God to take care of whatever, or whoever needs prayer at the moment. I try to talk to Him whenever and wherever and for no known reason, except that I just feel a need to talk to Him. I don't have to go to a special place, I don't have to get down on my knees, and I don't have to close my eyes to pray. Some of my best times with the Lord are when I am driving. I don't think He wants me to close my eyes.

For some reason people think they can't talk to God unless they are quiet, in a place by themselves, or in church. If you are a child of His, He will hear your requests whenever, wherever, and however you bring them to Him. I can be in the middle of a conversation and ask Him to help with the situation or to give me the words to say in response to someone's question. But when I am limited, by others, as to who can pray or why they can't be asked to pray I get stifled. If it's important enough to ask for prayer, why limit who can pray?

Sometimes someone whom I haven't seen or heard from for a long time will pop into my mind. Often times I will just say be with them Lord. When an ambulance goes screaming by I oftentimes, not always, just say take care of who or whatever is going on, be with them, be with the family.

If I am wrong Lord, please forgive me and show me the error of my thinking. Prayer is the one way we can be in touch with our God. It's one way we can receive answers to our questions. Prayer is one way we can bless Him and bless someone else. One way we can show love and concern for others, it's one way to feel close to Him.

More questions than answers but sometimes I only have questions. They just keep rolling around in my head. Why limit Him, why be afraid to let whoever feels the concern for someone else, be limited in their love for them by not letting them pray. So my thought is don't tell me the details just ask for unspoken requests, but don't limit who can pray. Am I wrong? if I am someone please let me know.

Have a great day and God bless!

Prayer of Jabez/ Blessing

Prayer of Jabez 1

Good morning:

I have been reading about Jabez, and the prayer he prayed.

> 1 Chronicles 4:10, "Jabez cried out to the God of Israel, 'Oh, that you would bless me, and enlarge my territory. Let your hand be with me, and keep me from harm, so that I will be free from pain! And God granted his request."

Little is known about this man, he is mentioned only in verses 9 & 10. His name, names were important back then, they represented what the child would be, means sorrowful, his mother bore him in sorrow. It can also mean pain.

So let's look at the prayer, first Jabez wanted God to bless him, but not bless him a little, he wanted God to bless him indeed. In those days indeed meant intensely or immensely.

Second, he asked that his territory be enlarged. So what does it mean to increase our territory; maybe in the area of the talents and gifts God gives us, more area to cover, more things that need doing, more people to teach, to increase our trust. We complain now about too much to do and not enough time to do it, perhaps we would have that time if we asked God to bless it.

Third, Jabez asked that God's hand would be with him. So do we ask God to be with us every minute of the day, I pray we do, but it is easy to let that little thought slip from us as we get busy with our day? This really means *be with me the way you choose*. So do we ask God to be with us at all times the way He chooses? Or are we looking for Him to be with us the way we choose?

Fourth, he asked that He would keep him from evil. We all want that, but do we do what scripture tells us to do to be kept in God's care. There are responsibilities we must accept as one of His children, Romans 12:9-21 tells us how. This is how we keep evil out and God in.

The prayer of Jabez is powerful, but it goes against what we have been taught. We have been taught to pray for others not ourselves, to ask for the needs of others and not for ourselves, But what if God wants us to ask for His blessings, for His guidance in our lives, for Him to be with us always, and that He keeps us from evil. The fact is *God does want us to ask for these things*. He is waiting to enlarge our territory, to be with us always. He wants us to quiet our hearts and minds so that we can hear His will for our lives. Not our will for our lives or what we think we want, but truly what His will is for our lives.

I challenge each of you to pray this prayer, *please bless me, the way you choose*. We get caught up in praying for the needs of everyone else. Pray for yourself, it's ok, it's not selfish, and it's asking God to be everything in your life. He sits waiting to be asked to bless us, so ask Him, you may be surprised at what you may receive from Him.

The territory of every Christian should be the heart, and the blessing lies in an increasing knowledge and intimacy with God. When our heart capacity for Him increases in our lives an entire family may be saved, a neighborhood can be changed, a church can see revival, and a community can be changed. Pray for God to bless you and increase your territory as He chooses. The last sentence says and God blessed him. In Romans 12: 9-21 Paul tells us how to do it.

See if we don't find more compassion, wisdom, mercy, hope joy and most of all more faith. Jabez prayed a short prayer and little is known about him, but the prayer he prayed was powerful. We need to add it to our prayers everyday and see what happens to us and those around us.

Have a great day and God bless you!

Prayer of Jabez 2

Good morning:

Yesterday I talked about and challenged you to pray the prayer of Jabez. Now some of you may have a hard time thinking it is okay to pray for blessings for yourself. But Jesus told us to pray for these things, it is biblical to do it, however, you may want to add that as the last part of your daily prayer time.

> Matthew 7:7-8, "Ask, and it will be given to you; seek, and you will find; knock, and the door will be opened to you. For everyone who asks, receives, and he who seeks, finds, and to him who knocks, the door will be opened."

He is not speaking just to those who need to find Him, but also to those who already know Him as savior.

> James 4:2-3, "You want something but don't get it. You kill and covet, but you cannot have what you want. You quarrel and fight. You do not have because you do not ask God. When you ask, you do not receive. Because you ask with wrong motives, that you may spend what you get on your pleasures."

All things are made by God, all things come from God and God loves to give them away. We need to ask with the right attitude. He doesn't just give to a few, He has enough blessings to give everyone as many as they ask for. As a father, mother, aunt, uncle, or grandparent, you give as much as you can to your children/grandchildren, niece or nephew, but the things should not be given if they are demanded. So what makes you think God doesn't want to give you what you ask for? His love is greater than anything we could imagine and he wants to give it to us all the time. God gives His blessings for nothing to both the saved and the unsaved, just because of His loving heart, but, some of His greatest blessings are reserved for those who ask.

Matthew 7: 9-11, "Which of you, if his son asks for bread, will give him a stone? Or if he asks for a fish, will he give him a snake? If you then, though you are evil, know how to give good gifts to your children, how much more will your Father in heaven give good things to those who ask Him?"

God wants us to ask for blessings and to seek greater encounters to serve Him. The phrase *Lord, bless me indeed,* is a personal prayer. We can ask for the needs of others, and then we need to ask for ourselves. He will bless us but if we ask He will bless us more abundantly.

The prayer is not specific, it is general. *You are allowing God to define, direct, and determine the blessing and how it will occur.* You are not putting qualifications on the request; you are leaving it totally up to God. The prayer doesn't ask for meager provision, but for abundant blessings. He gives us everyday what we need, what He wants us to do is ask for something He doesn't already give us. The greater our passion or desire, the more God loves to bless us. The prayer doesn't limit the request to a specific time, like today, it allows God to bless whenever, wherever, and however He prefers.

Sometimes we limit God because we put a time limit on when we want it, God's timing is perfect, and ours is not because we can't see the future. Some prayers need a time limit, but this prayer does not. It is for God to bless us, the way He sees fit, when the time is right and in the manner that is best for us. It is in His hands, we are just asking for blessings.

This prayer then is not a weak one, it is a fervent desire. A desire for God to bless us! It is an exuberant, adrenaline pumping request. It should not be asked in a meek, half hearted manner. It should be asked for with hunger and urgency. This is a prayer from your heart to God. From a child to his Father!

Again I challenge you to say the prayer. Find it in 1 Chronicles 4: 9-10.

God bless and have a great day!

Prayer of Jabez - three

Good morning:

Friday I sent you a second thought on the Jabez prayer. Today I am going to give you four things to do when you ask for His blessings.

- *Pray for God's blessings every day.* God wants us to ask Him to give us His blessings all the time.

When we pray it is usually for someone else, or a need we heard about, We need to ask God to bless our day and the things and people we encounter,. Watch for the blessings, recognize them and thank Him for them.

- *Thank God for His many blessings often.* Not a general thanks, but for specific blessings.

For instance, Friday night I had walked outside with Don when he went to work. When I went back into the house, we have three steps up into the house, on the inside; I stepped onto the middle step and turned around to lock the door. As I turned all my weight was on my right leg, the one I had surgery on, as I put my weight on it I realized my foot was only on the step about a 1/2 inch. There is no earthly reason that my foot should have stayed on that step instead of slipping off and going down hard on that leg to the bottom step, but it stayed right there on the middle step. I sent a special thank you to God; because that is the only reason I didn't go bang. It may seem like a small thing, but to me it was a blessing from my God who cares for me and watches over me all the time.

- *Enjoy God's blessings.* In Timothy 1 and 2 Paul is instructing Timothy in leadership.

1 Timothy 6: 17, "Command those who are rich in this present world not to be arrogant nor to put their hope in wealth, which is

so uncertain, but to put their hope in God, who richly provides us with everything for our enjoyment."

The thought comes to mind as we recognize the blessings God gives us, I don't deserve this; you are right, none of us deserve the blessings He gives us. They are gifts from your Heavenly Father who enjoys giving you what you need, so just enjoy them. But don't do as some do and say one day the shoe is going to fall, you can only receive so many good things before the bad will come. They are always looking for the bad and not enjoying each blessing as it comes to them. They don't fully trust their God.

- *Share your blessings with others.* God wants us to enjoy His blessings, but He also wants us to share them with others.

Sometimes when He says share the blessings it is for us to give something we especially hold dear to someone else. That may be to teach us that God asks for the very thing we hold on to so tightly.

God's gifts may be different than we think. They may come in relational form, or they may be spiritual or they may even be in material form or perhaps something else entirely. But they will be good because they came from the King, the Father who loves to give His children blessings.

Bruce Wilkinson has written a book called *The Prayer of Jabez.* I really enjoy the book. I have read it at least four times in the past 20 years. I have found it very encouraging and have prayed the prayer many times, although not daily, I can see the Blessings God has in store for us.

I believe when we seek God's blessing as the ultimate value in our life, we are throwing ourselves entirely into the path of His will and power and purpose for us. All our other needs become secondary to what we really want; which is to become completely immersed in what God is trying to do in us, through us, and around us so others can see His glory.

Have a Jesus filled day and God bless!

23RD PSALM

Good morning:

It is a dreary, cool, wet November day in S.E. Texas. On days like this it is hard to get excited about the day. It's a day that no matter how much you have to do, all you want is to sit curled up with a good hot drink and a good book. But, alas, most of us can't do that. Our day is usually already planned for us. Our schedules are full, there are difficult issues of life that have to be dealt with, and there are obstacles ahead of us we don't even know about. Such is the day of most of us. But we can become refreshed when we remember the 23rd Psalm. Most of us know it. It is often used at funerals, but it is actually intended for the living.

> Psalm 23: 1-3, "The Lord is my Shepherd; I shall not be in want. He makes me lie down in green pastures, He leads me beside quiet waters, and He restores my soul. He guides me in paths of righteousness for his name sake."

Yes, when our day is hectic, full of stress, we just need to go to Him and He will give us this peace. He will calm our frustrated mind and we can feel His presence within us.

> 4,"Even though I walk through the valley of the shadow of death, I will fear no evil, for you are with me."

We walk every day in a valley of death, that's what the world has to offer us. When we go out into our work places and into the hectic world of today we need to have God's protection before we leave our safe havens. He is always with us leading us through the valley. The valley may also be an unknown situation you have to face. We need to know that He is going with us and He will be there to protect us from this evil world.

> 4,"Your rod and your staff they comfort me."

God's promises and the word of our Lord comfort us. We just have to accept them and follow them and use them; they will comfort us when we need to be calm.

5,"You prepare a table before me in the presence of my enemies. You anoint my head with oil, my cup over flows."

When we are in the world we are in the presence of our enemies, they are all around us, the need for power, the need for more money, the need to be recognized as having done something great, and a host of other things. But when we take our Lord with us every day, He will give us the ability to overcome these enemies. He will give us direction, comfort, peace, and joy in their place. When He gives us all these every day our cup of spiritual blessings will overflow, He just keeps giving us more.

6,"Surely goodness and love will follow me all the days of my life, and I will dwell in the house of the Lord forever."

This is a promise, when we allow God to give us wisdom, knowledge, and understanding to deal every day with what we face, knowing He is there with us, walking every step beside us, or in some cases carrying us. His goodness and mercy will be there and we have the promise that we will, someday, be with Him forever.

It is comforting to know we can face whatever the day has to offer when we let Him guide us. His goodness is always with us, He desires for us to have joy, and He is always there to comfort us during the times we have to make difficult decisions. His strength is with us no matter what the challenges are.

So no matter what today holds in store for us, God is with us and will help us through the day. Even through these dreary, dark, wet days that lay ahead of us. We never have to face things alone. It only takes a phone call to someone you trust and you can be lifted up. After all that is what scripture tell us to do; to be there for our brothers and sisters.

I pray that even when the day is like today, dreary and cold; you can walk with the sunlight of God in your soul.

Have a great day and God bless!

Pride

Good morning:

The South Texas weather is so confusing, wait 10 minutes and it will change again. Life can be the same way. We get up in the morning thinking we know what the day is going to bring, but an hour into the day it takes a turn. An hour later it takes another turn. How do we keep up with all the changes in a day? We need to stay focused on the fact that no matter what happens in our lives each day we can depend on and trust God to guide us in every turn we come to.

Hebrews 13:5b, "I will never leave you or forsake you".

Jesus came in a human baby to show us that we could walk the way He did. He encountered every trial there was and showed us how to handle each one of them.

November has arrived and our lives will be taking on more twists and turns for the next 2 months. There will be company parties, families will be getting together, there will be church programs, school programs, and the ever present rush to find the perfect gift for each of our loved ones. We can get so busy with life's little twists and turns we forget to take that little extra time in our prayer time each day. Time we need to take, especially now, in this time of rush, hurry, and confusion. We need to keep some of the ever present dangers in mind and pray that we are protected from them. With all the things that will be coming at us let's be sure to keep away from feeling proud.

Pray for the temptation against pride:

James 4:6;"But He gives us more grace. That is why Scripture says, God opposes the proud, but gives grace to the humble"

Paul was taking to the unsaved here, but I believe it applies to us also. We have to be careful not to let pride get in. Satan loves that and can use it to turn us in the wrong direction. It's easy when we are in a hurry and feel pressured for time to let that little five letter word in. When we give the word *pride* to God and ask Him to protect us from it we will see His hand working in and through our lives. With that grace we can see more clearly the things we need to do.

Another thing we need to pray for is *protection against the power of Satan,* another five letter word. When we are in charge of an activity or a program, we need to give it to God. If we don't and we don't pray for protection against the power of Satan, he can use our position to get pushy, and demanding of things and others we are working with.

We are warned not to lord our position with Him over one another. When we are in charge and we want things to be perfect we can become a little puffed up and want to *lord it over others.* We need to be careful in the way we treat people; we need to be careful how we use our authority. We need to be listening to others; they may have a good idea that makes things go better. We have to be careful of these two five letter words, pride and power.

At this time of year we need to pray for protection against possessions. It's human nature to want certain things. We can become so taken with trying to find just the right outfit to wear to that party, and in telling others the things we would like to receive, that we let these things control our day, our week, and perhaps our mind. Having what we want is also a human trait, and we have to receive protection against it.

Pray that things don't come between you and God. Pray that He will guard you from *greed* regarding possessions. Another five letter word.

During this time of year it is easy to let our desire for pleasure take over. What we need to be aware of is that worldly pleasures can lead us down a path we really don't want to be on. The company party is set up for us to have pleasure and enjoy what they are providing for us. It is also a thank you for the year's work. As Christians we need to remember that our pleasure comes from the wonderful gift God gave us, Jesus, not the pleasures of the world .It is ok to enjoy those company parties as long as they don't become the main focus for us. God gives us richly all things to enjoy.

I have given my teens three verses to memorize that I think apply to us as well:

Proverbs 16:25, "There is a way that appears to be right to a man, but in the end it leads to death."

Proverbs 4:23 "Above all else, guard your heart, for it is the well spring of life."

Psalm 18:2 "The Lord is my rock, my fortress and my deliverer; my God is my rock in whom I take refuge."

If we remember these things and pray for protection from pride, power, greed, possessions, and pleasure, God will walk with us through whatever the world can throw at us.

Lord, keep me from making the mistakes I'm most prone to when temptation comes. I confess that what I think is necessary, smart, or personally beneficial is so often only the beautiful wrapping on sin. So please keep evil far from me!

Have a great day and God bless you!

Redemption/ Transformation

Restored in the Lord

Good morning:

It's strange how things come to our minds from nowhere. This morning my thoughts are around the word restore. Webster says, restore is to return to a former or natural state, to bring back to health and strength.

You can almost go anywhere with a word like that. When I opened my computer this morning news of more flooding in Australia was at the top of the news. More devastation and deaths caused by a natural disaster. I'm sure the people of Australia are praying for the time when their lives will be restored to a former time, one with no flooding. Our country needs to be restored to a former time in it's history. I'm sure most of us can remember a time when we would like things to return to a former time.

Christ doesn't return us to a former place and time; He restores us, giving us reassurance of His love and His peace. He restores us to Him. He restored the nation of Israel several times, He didn't return them He restored them to Himself. To return would be to go back to what we were before an event. To restore is to bring back to health by a new means. The land will restore itself to new health after a natural disaster.

A nation has to change its course of action to be restored to a former, more loving, a more God fearing state. People have to be restored with the things of Christ. Restoration takes time, patience, and understanding. When an event takes place in our lives that causes us to stumble and in some instances fall, we have to ask, and then walk in a restored state before God and man. Things are always coming our way to cause us to stumble but we don't have to fall back into a former self. We have to be restored by our God to a higher level of understanding. The trials of life, great or small, are lessons to be learned. These lessons are to take us to a higher level of forgiveness, a higher level of love for others, and a higher level of light.

Ephesians 5 says to be imitators of God, as dearly loved children and live a life of love. This is the condition He wants to restore us to. We are to walk ever more closely with Him. He will restore us to a higher level when we walk in His light. We are His light to this world.

> Ephesians 5:2, "And live a life of love just as Christ loved us and gave himself up for us as a fragrant offering and sacrifice to God."

> Ephesians 5:8-10, "For you were once darkness, but now you are light in the Lord. Live as children of light (for the fruit of the light consists in all goodness, righteousness and truth) and find out what pleases the Lord."

We all stumble, it's what we do with the stumble that matters, do we let the stumble cause us to fall backwards or do we ask for help and rise above and beyond the stumble to something better? If we let the stumble cause us to fall backwards we fall into darkness once again. If we let the stumble mature us we wake up and Christ will shine in us. We have the choice, to either *return* to the darkness or to be *restored* to a new person.

God restores the land; He can restore us to the light. The time is short before His return to claim His people and take them to Him.

> Ephesians 5:15-21, "Be very careful, then, how you live, not as unwise but as wise, making the most of every opportunity, because the days are evil. Therefore do not be foolish, but understand what the Lord's will is. Do not get drunk on wine, which leads to debauchery. Instead, be filled with the Spirit. Speak to one another with psalms, hymns and spiritual songs. Sing and make music in your heart to the Lord, always giving thanks to God the Father for everything, in the name of our Lord Jesus Christ. Submit to one another out of reverence for Christ."

When he says, do not get drunk on wine, it is also a euphemism for getting caught up in the things of this world, because they will lead to a separation with God. Instead, feed on the things of God and what He has for you and you will remain in His light.

The world will throw all kinds of things at us, and as the time draws ever nearer those things will come faster and harder. We have to have the strength to stand firm in our love for Christ and His kingdom, we can't let Satan cause us to stumble and fall. That is what he is determined to do. God wants all men to come to Him and have the light shine in their lives. Satan, on the other hand, wants everyone to turn from God and become a *slave* to him. Good versus evil; it has been in the world since the beginning of time. We know that good will win in the end, but evil will have its day.

We have to stay in the word, stay strong together, help each other and stand firm in Christ. We have to become mature in Christ and hold those up that are still babes in Christ. We have the love, the peace, the joy of knowing Christ, we also have the hope and the knowledge that He will return and take us away from this world of evil. We should also want these same things for our families and our friends.

Pray hard and let Christ's light shine in you so they find the Lord for themselves and will be joining us in our life with Christ for eternity.

Have a great day and God bless!

Transformation through God's love

Good morning:

There is a new movie out, Transformer 3, where objects change into another form. Webster says to transform is 1) to change the form or appearance of; 2) to change the condition, character, or function of. Scripture tell us we are to be transformed into Christ's likeness.

> 2 Corinthians 3:18 "And we, who with unveiled faces all reflect the Lord's glory, are being transformed into His likeness with every increasing glory, which comes from the Lord, who is the Spirit."

When we accept Christ into our hearts and recognize Him as our Savior our eyes are no longer covered, we can now see the glory of God. We are to reflect that glory. Once we couldn't see, now we can. We should be able to reflect God's glory in our lives.

> Romans 12:2, "Do not conform any longer to the pattern of this world, but be transformed by the renewing of your mind. Then you will be able to test and approve what God's will is, His good, pleasing and perfect will."

Transformation is not magic, it doesn't happen instantaneously. It happens gradually as we spend time in Scripture, with other believers, and in applying God's teachings to our lives.

> 1 Corinthians 11:1, says, "Follow my example, as I follow the example of Christ".

Most of us would hesitate to say that. But we all know people who by their example, make us want to be more steadfast, more loving, more gentle, and more forgiving, in other words, by their life we want to be more like Christ.

Kay Ashwell

Transformation takes place in a Christian community or in the Christian life, it does not come from a white-knuckle obedience or in response to criticism and pressure to conform, but from the love that can be seen in another person's face. A Christian community, the church, should reflect the love, honesty, vulnerability and opportunity that are present in Christ. It should be a living example of what and who Christ is.

The church is the living body of Christ, or should be. It should be speaking the truth in love, showing the compassion of Christ, reaching out to the hurting, the lost, the grieving, and the forgotten. The church should reflect the very image of God. This is done through the body, you and me. That does not mean that interactions with everyone will be sunshine and roses, but when we share a common commitment to Christ it should reflect Him.

> Romans 12:18-19, "If it is possible, as far as it depends on you, live in peace with everyone. Do not take revenge my friends, but leave room for God's wrath, for it is written, 'It is mine to avenge; I will repay says the Lord'".

Peace with others takes effort, it takes Christ living in you to be able to find peace with others.

Many people find it hard to believe God loves them until they feel love from others. Until they feel security in the body. The church, at its best, should reflect Christ's love and acceptance of others. It should accept people just as they are and let God do the work in their lives of transforming them.

I had a friend, whom I met in Jr. High, who lived in a dysfunctional home. Her mother was in a mental hospital, and had been for several years. Her dad was raising her, but he liked to drink too much. He did provide a roof over her head, not a nice one, but a roof anyway, and kept just enough food in the house so she wouldn't starve. She didn't know how to dress, how to keep her hair clean, how to keep her clothes clean. She was for all purposes left on her own to figure things out.

She started coming to our church one summer when we were having outdoor activities. She lived just a couple of blocks away from the church. Some of the kids ignored her and wouldn't have anything to do with her because she was dirty and her clothes were not clean and were not ironed. But a couple of us took her under our wings, so to speak, and showed her how to do things. Our mothers helped her learn how to fix meals, how to wash clothes and how to take care of herself.

She and I were very good friends all through school and into college where she met and married a man who became a pastor. She matured to become a pastor's wife and lived a full life. Why? Because a few people in the body of Christ, the church, showed her love, understanding, and fellowship, she was accepted just as she was. A few reflected Christ to her and she grew and matured in Him. She found a Father she could depend on, *a heavenly Father.*

Christians and the church have to come to the same understanding today. There are many out there who need someone to love them, someone to understand what they are going through, and someone to walk the next mile and take the next step with them. Every group of believers and every single believer has the power and the knowledge to show someone else who Christ is, what He can do for them, and how their life can become a reflection of Him. But it has to start with loving hearts, loving Christians, willing to put forth the effort to be Christ like.

We can't hide our faith under a barrel, or a bed, we have to let it shine as a light for others to see. The church has to stop being a closed building and open it up wide so others can see the love and forgiveness of Christ. Churches and Christians have to stop hiding that light and start letting it shine forth in this dark evil world. They have to stop being afraid, stop being apathetic and start to show the love of Christ.

Scripture is full of how we are to live our life so others can see; it is full of how to be able to walk as Christ walked in this world. It is full of how to live a holy life acceptable to God, but if we don't get into the word, if we don't get out of our little comfortable boxes, and if we don't uncover the light in us and in the church, others won't see Him or His love and mercy and forgiveness for them. They won't get to know Him. We will be held accountable on the Day of Judgment.

Let your light shine before men so they may see God through you and the way you live. A transformed life is one in which Christ lives, one in which He can work, one in which others can see Christ.

So be transformed into Christ's likeness and let it shine.

Have a great day and God bless!

To be restored

Good morning:

What a nasty, wet, rather cool morning we have here in SE Texas. It reminds me of some people's lives. They live and breathe in this world and have no hope of anything better. They just give in to what the world throws at them. They don't know there is a way to see beyond the storms of life. They don't know they can be rescued from the storm. They don't know Jesus can redeem them.

Redeem, in Webster, is to get or buy back; to pay off; to turn in for premiums; to ransom; to deliver from sin; to fulfill; to make amends for or atone for; to restore to favor.

That pretty much says who Jesus was and is. If you never thought about Jesus in that light before now is a good time. He came to get us back in touch with the Father. He came to pay off our debt of sin owed to God. He came to turn us from nothing in God's eyes to a premium child. He came to ransom us from this evil world. He came to deliver us from the sins we had committed. He came to fulfill the love that God has for His creation. He came to atone for our evil lives. He came to restore us to a place of honor in our Father's world. Yes, Jesus is truly our Redeemer.

Psalm 130: 1-8, "Out of the depths I cry to you, O Lord; O Lord hear my voice. Let your ears be attentive to my cry for mercy. If you, O Lord, kept a record of sins, O Lord who could stand? But with you there is forgiveness; therefore you are feared. I wait for the Lord, my soul waits, and in His word I put my hope. My soul waits for the Lord more than watchmen wait for the morning. O Israel put your hope in the Lord, for with the Lord is unfailing love and with Him is full redemption. He Himself will redeem Israel from all their sins."

Kay Ashwell

Fear of God is not being afraid of Him physically, it is coming to understand His glory; to see Him as above everything else; no one is equal to Him; and it is the beginning of wisdom, trust, and confidence.

Israel is all of God's people. We have been given the keys to life evermore, to live in a world of peace and love with our Father as His child. We can have confidence that whatever has happened in the past or what may come to pass in the future it is in the hands of our Father. That confidence comes from trusting in God. The world doesn't have this confidence because they have not yet learned to trust God. Nothing in this world is certain, but the person who trusts in God is never disappointed. Every obstacle is an opportunity for God to show His power, every difficulty is a way to learn from Him and know His comfort.

Even though the storms of life assault us and try to break our confidence and our will; we will be able to stand firm because God has called us to a better life; to a restored life with Him. We know that we are constantly in his care. Let's never miss an opportunity to try and bring others into this same confidence and trust. It's our calling when we are redeemed by our Savior and Lord.

Have a great day and God bless!

To be hot for God

Good morning:

Apathy, what does that word bring to mind? To Webster it means, "Without emotion, lack of emotion, indifference, listlessness." Revelation tells us what God calls apathy; He is talking to the church in Laodicea.

> Revelation 3:15-17; "I know your deeds, that you are neither cold nor hot. I wish you were either one or the other! *So because you are lukewarm, neither hot nor cold, I am about to spit you out of my mouth.* You say I am rich; I have acquired wealth and do not need a thing. But you do not realize that you are wretched, pitiful, poor, blind and naked."

We, the people who attend a church, are the church, and yes it is talking to each of us.

Take a look around, the world is in the grip of Satan and his workers. Our country, even though it is supposed to be a Christian nation, is under Satan's control. This nation and the people in it, including a majority of Christians, are in a state of *apathy*. We are neither hot nor cold; we just keep going along with the flow. Never standing up and being heard.

We seem to think that God is going to take care of everything in His own time. He will, but only under the condition that we become active and start giving Him the praise and glory that He deserves. Only when we wake up and come out of our *apathy* will He be able to rebuild our lives and the life of this country.

We are the light in this world of darkness. Other peoples and nations look to us for hope. How can we give them hope when we don't show any interest in it? Just let us be and don't bother us with details, is what most people think. Just let me do what I want all week and on Sunday, if there isn't anything going on, I'll come to church and say thank you Lord for what you have given me. This is being neither hot nor cold as scripture tells us. This scripture is a warning from God, either get hot or get cold. Otherwise, He is about to spit us out of His mouth.

If you read on in that scripture it continues:

> Revelation 3:18, "I counsel you to buy from me gold refined in the fire, so you can become rich; and white clothes to wear, so you can cover your shameful nakedness; and salve to put on your eyes, so you can see."

God has provided for us the things we need to follow His directions for our lives. He has given us His word, the Bible, but if we don't pick it up and read it we can't find the riches He promised. He has provided for us forgiveness so our sins and evil ways can be taken away and we can wear white robes. He has given us the Holy Spirit who was sent to show us all truth so our eyes will be opened, but if we don't learn how to listen to Him we will remain in the dark.

> Revelation 5: 10-21, "Those whom I love I rebuke and discipline. So be earnest, and repent. Here I am, I stand at the door and knock, if anyone hears my voice and opens the door, I will come in and eat with him, and he with me. To him who overcomes, I will give the right to sit with me on my throne, just as I overcame and sat down with My Father on His throne."

There is hope but we have to take the steps it takes to let it happen; not only in our own life, but in the life of the church and the country.

Jesus went to Golgotha, he was hanged on a tree, nails were driven in his hands and feet they put a crown of thorns on him. He was flogged, it was a cruel time. Jesus is with us in modern day, but He is not called on, He is ignored and people say they don't need Him. But He still says to His *Father; forgive them, for they know not what they dong.* Luke 23: 34

It's time to wake up and get on with the business that God has called us to do. We can no longer ride the fence, hopping to the right when it looks good and hopping to the left when something over there looks pleasing. We have to walk the path God has given us to walk.

So decide today if you are going to be with God or if you are going to continue to jump left and right as things look appealing. You have to be either hot or cold for God; you cannot be both and make it into eternity with Him.

When you make that choice I pray it will be *hot* for God, if it is and you truly want to let Him control your life, then let Him, He will give you the strength to face each day, to look the day in the eye and say, today is your day Lord, help me to do what you have for me today.

We and our country have to be redeemed!

Have a great day and God bless!

Sacrifice

Good morning:

We hear in church, and elsewhere, the word sacrifice. Have you given it much thought? Sacrifice in Webster is, an offering of a life or an object to a deity; a giving up of one thing for the sake of another; a loss incurred in selling something.

We all know, or should know, that Christ was the sacrificial lamb who was slain for each of us. Do you ever stop to think what that really means? Let's look at Genesis 22:1-18, it's the story of Abraham and Isaac. Remember that Abraham was 100 years old when God granted Abraham and Sarah their desire for a son. Isaac was an only son. When Isaac was in his teens God called on Abraham to sacrifice him as a burnt offering.

Genesis 22: 1-18:

> Verse 2 God told Abraham, "take your only son, Isaac, whom you love, and go to the region of Mariah; sacrifice him there as a burnt offering on one of the mountains I will tell you about."

Did Abraham argue with God? Did he try to figure out what he could do to keep his son? No, it tells us he took his son, wood for the offering, a fire starter and a knife and the two of them headed up to the mountain. Not only was Abraham going to obey God, without question, he had to travel some distance to come to the place that it was to be done, giving him plenty of time to think and possibly change his mind and ignore God.

Abraham gives his son an answer to the question where is the lamb?

> Genesis 22: 7-8, "Isaac spoke up, and said to his father Abraham, 'Father,' 'Yes, my son!' Abraham replied.

'The fire and wood are here,' Isaac said, 'but where is the lamb for the burnt offering?' Abraham answered; 'God himself will provide the lamb for the burnt offering my son.' And the two of them went on together."

Abraham and Isaac went on to where God told him, and they built the altar; Abraham bound his son and laid him on the altar. He was going to do what God was asking him to do. Abraham was being tested. Abraham proved faithful and at the last moment God called to Abraham and told him not to lay a finger on Isaac. As Abraham looked up he saw a young sheep caught in some bushes and the lamb was offered in place of Isaac. Abraham was faithful in his love and devotion to God. He was willing to sacrifice his only son, whom he didn't have until he was an old man, if that was what God asked him to do.

This act was symbolic to what God would give the world; His only Son who was sacrificed on the cross for our sins. *Jesus became the sacrificial lamb for each of us.*

So why is it so hard for us to sacrifice the little things God asks us to give up? God is not going to ask us to sacrifice one of our children; he will ask us to sacrifice other less necessary things to prove our love for Him. Things like pride, selfishness, self-centeredness, anger, resentment, money, your time, those cigarettes, that beer, or whatever else is standing in the way of you being able to give your whole self to Him.

God wants all of you, not just a part of you. He wants you to turn everything over to Him. He sacrificed His only Son so that we would be able to come to Him pure and holy. Not with a lot of baggage around our necks. If Abraham and God were willing to give up the most precious thing they had, we should be able to give up the little things in our lives that hinder our walk with God. You have to be willing to give them over to God and let Him take care of them. We have to give Him our loved ones and trust He will provide them with what is best for them. We have to be willing to give up the little things for a closer walk with Him.

Kay Ashwell

Philippians 2:13-15; "for it is God who works in you to will and to act according to his good purposes. Do everything without arguing, so that you may become blameless and pure children of God without fault in a crooked and depraved generation, in which you shine like stars in the universe."

When we are willing to give up the small things in our lives to Him, He will provide us with the strength and power to overcome the big things in our lives. So we can walk with him with a pure heart. He gave the ultimate sacrifice, so we could learn to obey and follow him.

Many people get hung up on the idea of how can I serve Him. I don't have anything to give Him that is worth anything. That's not true, you have yourself, all of you, which is what God wants. He just wants you to come to Him and to follow what He has given you. He doesn't want you to worry over things of this world. He doesn't want you to worry about having the strength to do what needs to be done. He doesn't care if you have a beautiful voice, good looks, or if you are smart or talented. He doesn't want you to fret over your faults or weaknesses or worry about tomorrow. He only cares about how much you love Him and are willing to follow what He is asking you to do. He will provide all the things that are necessary for you to accomplish your tasks. He will accomplish amazingly good things through you. He wants true hearts that love Him.

Turn everything over to Him and don't take them back, walk in the light He has given you; trust Him to provide the things you need to remain in Him.

Romans 8:28, "And we know that in all things God works for the good of those who love Him, who have been called according to His purpose."

He has a purpose for each of us. Let Him lead you into what that purpose is. May God strengthen your hearts in every good work, word and deed!

Have a great day and God bless!

Spiritual Strength

Spiritual Strength in being thankful

Good morning:

As I arise this morning, I am reminded how wonderfully God created this earth and each of us. I am teaching from Genesis and as I study and prepare for each class, He reminds me that there was a special purpose in His creation.

Just to think that each of us is God's special creation leaves me in awe. He knows everything about us, He knows how each piece of our body was formed, He knows each brain cell we have and He knows how we will use them. Let's stop a moment and consider the fact that our bodies and our minds were knit together by Him for a purpose. We may think we have flaws that we can't do what we want because we don't have that special ability. But God didn't make a mistake when He formed us. He formed us to do certain things in this world. The things we may see as flaws in our self are actually His special mark on our life. These flaws, as we see them, He uses in a powerful way to make Himself known to us.

He made us in His image and He intends for us to use what He has given us to serve and fulfill the tasks He sets before us, tasks which seem overwhelming in this present world. He gave us what we call flaws to remind us each day that He is with us. That He will never leave us. Just as each day is new and fresh, so is our task each day new and fresh.

When we have Jesus as our pilot our day can stay fresh. I hope each of you awakens to the peace He gives us. Each morning the sun comes up, the birds sing, the waters flow, they are constant, but fresh each day. Our lives should be the same. Paul gives us in Philippians 4 the secret of peace and sufficiency. He intends for us the very best He can give.

> Philippians 4:5-7, "Rejoice in the Lord always, I will say it again, rejoice; let your gentleness be evident to all.

The Lord is near. Do not be anxious about anything, but in everything by prayer and petition, with thanksgiving, present your requests to God. And the peace of God, which transcends all understanding, will guard your hearts and your minds in Christ Jesus."

When He created man in His image, He wanted a people who He could walk among, who He could commune with, and a people who would love Him as much as He loves them. If we think we have no other purpose in life than to just believe in Him we are missing the true joy of knowing Him. He has a purpose for us each day and it is our responsibility to fulfill that purpose. He is there to help us through the day, to give us guidance, wisdom, and the ability to accomplish the tasks set before us. We have to take the responsibility of being who He called us to be so that purpose can unfold each day. We have to say thank you Lord for my life, for my flaws, and then say ok today is new and fresh what is it we, He and I, are to accomplish today?

My mother, who is 92 years old and blind, says to her Lord every morning *"thank you for giving me another day, now what are we going to do with it?"* She could get up and do nothing but sit and feel sorry for herself. Her sight has been gone for the past dozen years. She could be very discouraged and feel worthless. She doesn't, she gets up expecting the day to be good and she sets about making it that way. She says God is not letting me forget He made me for a purpose and each day I have a chance to fulfill that purpose. It may be to only be a good listener, or to have a positive word for someone who doesn't know His love. But He has given me a new day and I will use it to the best of my ability. I tell her you are His prayer warrior, and you are good at it.

Note to reader: Since this was written several years ago, my mother got called home at the wonderful age of 99 ½ years. She served God every day in some way.

We should all look at life with our Lord that way. It would make this world a better place, one moment at a time, each person giving their best to the Lord. Your responsibility may be to pray for a certain thing, it may be to smile at a stranger, it may be to give an encouraging word to someone, but there is a purpose for each of us each day. When we allow Him to use us that purpose is being met.

May the peace of our Lord fill you today, may you feel His love for you and as the dawn turns to day and the day turns to night may you know you have been in His care all day long.

Have a great day and God bless!

Spiritual Strength through prayer

Good morning:

A tidbit before I start my thought for the day, have you taken a good look at the October calendar? Did you notice that there are 5 Friday's, 5 Saturdays, and 5 Sundays this month?

One other thing about calendars, we fill them up with things to do each day. Many carry an organizer or have one in their phone, with things that have to get done each day. What is the first thing you have listed on that organizer?

We have challenges every day and we feel the necessity to organize our day, hour by hour so we don't miss anything that needs to get done. Even in retirement or semi-retirement we feel the need to organize our day. In the world today our phones, computers and organizers keep us busy every day. Because of these things in our lives we can no longer get away from the business of the day. We can't even get away from it in our vehicles, since we carry our phones with us.

Since my surgery I have had to take a second look and rearrange my mind and thinking, first from just getting through the day in the first days after surgery, to being able to motivate with some ease as it went into weeks, and now four months later my mind is ready to make daily plans, but my body is still not accommodating me. I still have to depend on help to accomplish some things. Oh, don't get me wrong, I thank God for the healing that has taken place, I am far ahead of where most are at this time, but I am still limited in what I can do. For someone who was always on the go, it has taken some adjustment. As those of you who have daily schedules pursue your day and get it all done, I have to get used to the fact that even though I schedule things to do each day, I don't get them all done.

I think we all need to stop and consider that perhaps our daily schedules are planned in our flesh, worldly needs or concerns. So back to my

Kay Ashwell

original question, what is the first thing on your daily schedule? Do you have God at the top of the day or at the bottom of the day? As Christians we should have Him at the top and the bottom of our list. He is the one who can get us through the day and accomplish the things we need to do, and He should be the one we thank at the end of each day. He may have something else in mind for us to do that day. Are we ready to meet and accomplish what He has in mind for us?

We may think we are headed in the right direction and following the right path, but do we let God lead us in all we say and do each day? Or do we just head out the door and push through the day and then say thank you Lord for getting me through the day after it is all done?

If we are not careful and prayerful with our day, we may find ourselves agreeing with the world, I got all the things done I needed to do. Good for you, you got it all done, but is it what God wanted done through you? God's daily planner for our lives may be entirely different than ours. I have had to learn to lean on Him to get anything accomplished. What He has in store for me every day may not be exactly what I have in mind to accomplish. I have had to slow down, rest, and am thankful that I am able to do anything on my own without help. He gives me help through loving, caring friends. But He also has given me time to just be with Him. Time I have learned to accept with thankfulness.

Psalm 105 gives us God's "daily planner," do we put these things in our organizers?

> Psalm 105: 1-4; "Give thanks to the Lord, call on his name; make known among the nations what he has done. Sing to him, sing praise to him; tell of all his wonderful acts. Glory in his holy name; let the hearts of those who seek the Lord rejoice. Look to the Lord and his strength; seek his face always."

Among the things He has planned for us is to give thanks to Him, call on Him, let others know what He has done for us, sing praises to Him, tell of His wonderful love, let those who seek Him rejoice, look to Him for strength, seek Him always, remember His miracles and His judgment. You may be thinking, I don't need to put those things on my organizer, but you do, if they are not there for you to see, we have a tendency to leave them out of our day. It is human and common for us to get so busy doing what we need to do we forget to do the things God has planned for us. We need to consider these things every day so we can remember to do them.

What a difference it may make in someone's life if we just smile at them, tell them God loves them, open a door for them, say a kind word, be patient with them, don't show any anger or frustration when they are ahead of us and are slow or frustrated themselves. Our response to them, our attitude toward them may be the only positive thing in their day. Will they remember it? You bet they will, and it may cause them to want to know how we can respond with kindness and grace in trying situations and that gives us the chance to tell them how Jesus helps us thorough our day. How He gives us the peace and love we need to just get through a day in this world.

We have the privilege of consulting with Him, the King of Kings, to determine what path we will take, what tasks are most important, and who needs us the most. Are we willing to let Him be in control of what we encounter each day?

Have a great day and God bless!

Spiritual Strength through patience

Good Morning;

This is a little later than usual, I guess I needed sleep bad enough that God saw to it that I slept, and I praise Him for that as I have felt a little worn out of late.

The *Big Picture of life* comes to mind today. What is the Big Picture' in your life? Is it getting up each day to the tedium of the day? Go to work and come home and work at home. Is it wondering when you will have that day off to just do nothing? Is it in wishing your life was different and things would go the way you want? Is it getting up and saying ok Lord we have a new day, what are we going to do today that will glorify you.? My days are pretty much the same, but the first thing I do every day, usually at 5am but sometimes 7am, is to say, as I sit down at this computer, what is it you want me to write today? Sometimes it comes so fast I hardly have time to type it, other days it comes a little slower and I have to search Scripture to put it all together. But the pleasure it gives me can't be measured or said in words. So what about your day?

I'm going to tell you a story today of a time most won't remember anything about, it happened during WW Il, most of you were not born yet or you were just a baby or small child. Most men were in the military serving in one area of the world or another. The duties here at home were left to the women and older children, that included factory work which made the things the men needed. There were many factories making the same things to support the troops but one of the factories that made parachutes is what I'm going to tell you about.

I sew and I love to make things, but to sit 10 hours a day sewing together pieces of cloth that didn't resemble anything and that was without color would have been tedious, boring and dull even to me. So this one factory, every morning before they started the day's work, held a meeting and the workers were told approximately how many parachutes had been strapped onto the backs of pilots, copilots, and other 'flying' personnel the previous day. They were told approximately how many men had jumped to safety from disabled planes, and how many had jumped into the fighting. The managers of the factory encouraged the workers to see the *big picture* of what they were doing. The importance of the job they were doing. As a second means of motivation, the workers were asked to form a mental picture of a loved one or friend that might be the one saved by the parachute they were sewing. I don't need to tell you that the level of quality from that factory was one of the highest on record; the workers had the *big picture* in front of them every day.

Why, because they were given a reason to make the parachutes perfect every morning. God wants us to strive for perfection too. We can't let the tedium of each day become only stitching that means nothing. We have to keep our eyes on the big picture; the picture Christ set before us, eternity with Him.

Instead of seeing each day as just another day to get through, focus on the people you may help, the ones who need a friendly touch. Focus on why you do what you do and who will benefit from your work. You will be touching the lives of people you don't even know or may never meet. No matter what your job is there is always a *big picture*, bigger than you realize day to day. You may not know the answer as to why you are where you are at the moment, but God does and He will see you carry out His big picture when we allow Him to lead us each day.

It takes practice and patience to perform the tasks God sets before us, let us not get weary in carrying them out. We need to persevere so we can be with God in eternity. To reach the state of perfection that all our patience and practice has brought us. No matter what the task is for today, see it as an opportunity to accomplish one more thing for the Lord and get us one step closer to eternity.

We won't be called home until we have accomplished the tasks God has set before us. We can have a glimpse of eternity when we let God lead us each day and we come to the end of the day with peace, joy, and love in our hearts. Nothing can give us more peace and joy than passing on the love of God to someone else.

So today and each day arise with one thought, Lord what are we going to accomplish for your kingdom today? Go about your day with Him leading and guiding you and at the end of the day you will be able to look back and say thank you Lord for this beautiful day you gave me. Do each task as if you are doing it for God, because ultimately you are. Jesus said when you do these things for the least of my brothers you do them to Me. Keep the big picture in front of you, always.

Have a great day and God bless!

Spiritual Strength through knowledge

Good morning:

Another Monday morning, how do you feel today? Have you already asked for God's help? Thanking Him for a good night's rest. Thanking Him for the day ahead. Those should be your first thoughts of the day. With His help you can accomplish all you are to do today and still have time to meditate on the things of His which you should be doing.

> Colossians 1:10, "We pray this in order for you to live a life worthy of the Lord and please Him in every way; bearing fruit in every good work, growing in the knowledge of God."

Increasing in His knowledge is the key to living a full life in and through Him. The world today says I can do it myself. If you think that way this morning you are lost before you begin. No one can do anything without the Lord's help. When we try, we make a mess of it all. Our lives get so confused and disoriented that we feel like we just can't take another step forward.

Life is like a tree. It has lots of roots running in all directions in search of nutrients and water. They are close to the surface so they can get every bit they can find. They are long and small. They gather every ounce of nutrients around them but they are not satisfied, so they grow longer and search farther from the tree. If these long surface roots are all the tree has it eventually won't be able to hold the tree firm in a wind storm. The tree will topple over, it can't stand if its roots are too shallow. A tree which puts down a tap root that goes deep into the ground in search of nutrients and water builds a strong root system. The arterial roots that go out from it are stronger because they don't have to travel so far to find what they need. They are thicker and shorter. When the winds and storms come they can hold the tree firm because they go deeper and are stronger, able to withstand the wind.

Kay Ashwell

Life is like that; when we think we can do things on our own we run from here to there in search of the things we need, never taking the time to settle into any long lasting understanding. We grow weary of the struggle to survive in this world. But, when we take the time to read, listen and hear, the nourishment that we need, what our Lord is saying, when we put into practice those things that give us strength, we can withstand the winds of life which come our way.

By reading Scripture, attending church, being around other Christians, and most of all being in communication with God, we grow strong tap roots that go deep into our souls and make us strong. So when the storms and trials and difficult times come we will be able to stay strong and tall, not giving into the winds that blow.

> Proverbs 2:6-8, "For the Lord Gives wisdom, and from His mouth come knowledge and understanding. He holds victory in store for the upright; He is a shield to those whose walk is blameless, for he guards the course of the just and protects the way of the faithful ones."

In our modern culture, Christians have to seek out spiritual food that will give us spiritual maturity. We need regular time of prayer and Bible study, individual and corporate worship, serving others and Christian fellowship, to help us grow. So what is the benefit of building a strong taproot, is it the benefit of depth in our spiritual life?

In John 15:1-12, Jesus is talking about the vine and the vine dresser. The vine is Jesus the vine dresser is God. Jesus says that the leaves, us, and the fruit, what we accomplish, cannot survive without the vine which is attached to the trunk. We cannot go through life without Jesus and God to keep us strong and healthy, growing and producing fruit.

Superficiality is the way of the world. What people need today is not a large amount of those who think they are intelligent, or a group who feel they have all the answers, but they need people who have a deep strength. People who have set their lives deep in the Scriptures, deep in Christ and can draw strength from Him.

Today draw from Him, draw closer to Him, determine in your mind that it is through Him that you will be able to withstand the winds, the problems, the challenges which lie ahead. The winds will come, are you building the strong taproot that will enable you to remain firmly planted? If not, I would suggest that this becomes your goal. Grow stronger in the Lord and let Him help you weather the storms of life.

Have a great day and God bless!

Spiritual Strength in the Spirit

Good morning:

Matthew 5:3, "Blessed are the meek, for they will inherit the earth."

This is part of the first Beatitude Jesus spoke to the crowds who followed him. What does it really mean? It is not speaking of an attitude toward other people as it is to an attitude toward God, mainly humility. The earth is the new earth as in Revelation 21. My question is, do you have the whole Spirit with you, the right attitude toward God or are you content to accept what you have of it?

Look at those around you, are they poor in spirit? What do you do to try and fill them up with the Spirit? Do you encourage them; listen to what is going on in their lives? Do you pray with them? Christians can be poor in spirit as well as those who don't have the spirit. Do we see them as poor in Spirit also, or just think they are having an off day? Does knowing them rekindle anything in you?

We should realize that everyone needs to be fed each and every day to have the proper attitude toward God. That does not mean physical food, it means we need to be fed spiritual food; food that can sustain us for the long haul. We need to have a new understanding that when we do anything positive with or for others we are feeding something inside of them as well as feeding our own spiritual self.

People, even those in our own families, are hungry for something more beautiful, greater, and longer lasting than most people can give. Even though people won't admit it to themselves, or to others, they are hungry for God. They hunger for something to fill the void in their lives, to give them some peace and rest from the turmoil of life. Many Christians are hungry and they are suffering in one way or another, because they don't know how to reach this goal. They just go from day to day doing what has to be done and trying to do the right things, but they don't have that inner peace that a truly Spirit filled person has.

Today as we meet people remember they are hungry for something, and so say a prayer for them. Even if it is a stranger walking down the street you pass by, say a prayer for them. You won't know if it helped but God will and you will be blessed for saying it. If someone comes to your mind, call them up, they may need an encouraging word. When you do so you will feel the peace and contentment in your own soul. These are things we are expected to do. God has given us the Spirit so we can share it with others.

Some He called to preach or teach, others He called to be encouragers. We all have a responsibility to God and His kingdom when we have the Spirit, and that is to share it with others. It's really not hard to share God's love; you can do it with a smile, a kind word, an encouraging pat on the back, a silent prayer for someone or for many, a listening ear. It doesn't take much to pass on the love and peace of God to another. By so doing your Spirit will be fed as well.

> Philippians 3:12-16, 'Not that I have already obtained all this, or have already been made perfect, but I press on to take hold of that for which Christ Jesus took hold of me. Brothers, I do not consider myself yet to have taken hold of it. But one thing I do: Forgetting what is behind and straining toward what is ahead. I press on toward the goal to win the prize for which God has called me heavenward in Christ Jesus. All of us who are mature should take such a view of things, and if on some point you think differently, that too God will make clear to you. Only let us live up to what we have already attained."

It is the responsibility of those who are mature in Christ to bring those who are not along the path. A person can have gone to church all their lives and still be a babe in Christ. They may not have given themselves completely to God or they may be hanging on to something and not giving it up, whatever it is they are not mature in Christ and we have a responsibility to them as well as to the unsaved.

Today strive to be Christ to someone, somehow.

Have a great day and God bless!

Spiritual Strength through the word

Good Morning:

> Psalm 139:15. "My frame was not hidden from you
> when I was made in the secret place; when I was woven
> together in the depths of the earth.

The meaning is to the womb where it is dark, moist and unknown. God has created each of us and He has a plan for each of us. God knows the very heart of every man. See yourself as God sees you, He gave you your talents, your personality, your likes, He knows you inside out. Those details make you unique; they were chosen by God just for you.

How you use them is what makes the difference. We can thank Him by being who He designed us to be or we can separate ourselves from Him by letting the world control us. The difference between heaven and hell is the difference between good and evil, sin.

Paul, in Colossians 3 is telling us to let go of our weak character traits like anger, rage, malice, slander and filthy language, and put on good ones like compassion, kindness, humility, gentleness and patience. Most don't understand this; they think God expects them to change overnight once they have accepted Him as their savior. That's where they get into trouble; no one can change all their worldly habits over night. God knows that and doesn't expect anyone to change that quickly.

What He does expect and what we have to do is what Paul says in Colossians 3.

> Colossians 3:1-2. "Since then you have been raised with
> Christ, set your hearts on things above, where Christ
> is seated at the right hand of God. Set your minds on
> things above, not on earthly things."

We can't continue to think as the world thinks. The putting off the old and putting on the new begins in the mind with the determination to learn about, understand and be like Christ. We can't think or act like the world any longer, we have to focus on Christ and what He has promised us. We have to commit our day, each day, to the Father in prayer. We have to become familiar with the voice of the Holy Spirit by reading Scripture. And we have to *trust* that God will change us from the inside out. When He does, we will become new creatures, and others will notice the change.

When we become familiar with the voice of the Holy Spirit, and have given our day and our bad habits to God each hour, every day, in prayer we will start to see a change and that change will continue to increase and we will become more like Christ. God knows you can't do it in one day, although there are some who say they have experienced that dramatic change.

Most of us change over time, little by little. That's OK as long as we are making the changes we need to make each and every day. When the world and its evil pull us down, we don't have to start over, but we do have to ask for Gods' forgiveness. Each lesson we learn, each test we go through, each trial we face brings us closer to Him. We don't know what we are capable of doing until we try. If we never try we will never get past the first step.

God wants everyone to come to Him, but we also know that only a few will make it. Now a few in a multitude of trillions is many. You can be in that few. Be what God made you to be and accomplish what God intended you to accomplish in your life. Every part of you is lovely in the eyes of God. Make Him a proud Father by who you are becoming. So when the day comes and He calls us home He will say, "Well done, true and faithful servant." Matthew 25:21

Read Chapter 3 in Colossians today and learn how to become Holy as He is Holy; learn your Spiritual strength.

Have a great day and God bless!

Spiritual Strength through power

Good morning:

Today I am taking you to Colossians 2.

> Colossians 2: 6; "So than, just as you received Christ
> Jesus as Lord, continue to live in Him, rooted and built
> up in Him, strengthened in the faith as you were taught,
> and overflowing with thanksgiving."

Paul was explaining to them, and us, that they gain a new appreciation of Jesus as being the absolute fullness of God, and that He is the only power source for living the Christian life.

I read about a village in France, LeChambon, where during the German occupation of France in WW II residents hid the Jewish families in the village.

This village was so consecrated to the Lord that they did the ultimate for their neighbors; they were willing to risk their lives to save the lives of others. They had heard Sunday after Sunday about what was right and obtained the courage from God to do it. So on the day the Nazis came to town they just went about doing what was right. There was one lady who faked a heart attack when they came into her home so they wouldn't search it. This is what having the power of the Holy Spirit means. To know when we are in tune with the Lord, to know when we are following His directions, He will give us the courage, the power, and the desire to do what He would do. This is being *plugged* into His power. We don't have that power on our own; Christ gives it to us.

> Colossians 2:10. "And you have been given fullness
> in Christ, who is the head over every power and
> authority."

Kay Ashwell

We have to live a Christian life; there can be no cults, no philosophies, no hollow religions, no riding the fence in our walk. We have to have a victorious life, so when we are needed we are ready as God has prepared us to be. The people of LeChambon, France were *plugged* into Christ and were ready, willing and acted on what they had been taught. Wouldn't it be wonderful if the Christians in America would come together in such a manner? Can you imagine what this country would look like? Certainly it would not look the way it looks now.

What was true for them is true today. Having received Jesus as our Savior, we are given His Spirit from whom we receive guidance and direction; as we search the Scriptures, pray, and listen to His still small voice. Then we are *plugged* in to Him as our source and ultimate authority. In this Spirit we can influence our families, our neighbors, our friends, our church and our community.

Today let us get plugged in to the life God intended for us; the lives of obedience, love, joy, peace, and hope.

Not the life of timidity, being afraid to say or do anything for fear of offending someone. Jesus offended a lot of people, but He always did it to prove or teach a point that had to be taught. We are to be full of the Spirit, who has the power to help us be strong and sure of our faith and trust in Him. Not to be intimidated by some other force.

God bless and have a great day!

Spiritual Strength in God's promises

Good morning:

> Isaiah 50:4; "The Sovereign Lord has given me an instructed tongue, to know the word that sustains the weary. He wakens me morning by morning, wakens my ear to listen like one being taught".

Each morning he awakens me eager to learn his teaching. The message I seem to be getting this morning is one of spiritual and physical strength. There are so many things in the world today that try to drain us of our strength. When we are weak is when Satan can come in and cause havoc with our mind and spirit. We have to be strong in our walk with the Lord in order to overcome this. I'm going to take us back into the Old Testament and give you a few promises that God gave to Joshua when he had to take over leading the Israelites across the Jordan River into the Promised Land.

The first passage I want us to look at is Deuteronomy 31:7-8, where Moses is instructing Joshua.

> "Then Moses summoned Joshua and said to him in the presence of all Israel. 'Be strong and courageous, for you must go with this people into the land that the Lord swore to their forefathers to give them, and you must divide it among them as their inheritance. The Lord himself goes before you and will be with you; He will never leave you nor forsake you. Do not be afraid; do not be discouraged."

The second Scripture is. The Lord is speaking to Joshua in these verses after Moses died.

> Joshua 1:6-9 "Be strong and courageous, because you will lead these people to inherit the land I swore to their

forefathers to give them. Be strong and very courageous. Be careful to obey all the law my servant Moses gave you; do not turn from it to the right or to the left, that you may be successful wherever you go. Do not let this Book of Law depart from your mouth; meditate on it day and night, so that you may be careful to do everything written in it, then you will be prosperous and successful. Have I not commanded you? Be strong and courageous. Do not be terrified; do not be discouraged, for the Lord your God will be with you wherever you go."

There is a real message in these passages for us today. Joshua had been given a large task and God was encouraging him, giving him the same promises that had been given to Moses many years before and the same one Moses had given Joshua.

It's interesting to note that God specifically tells Joshua not to be terrified or discouraged. What was it that could have possibly "terrified" or "discouraged" Joshua? It was the physical size of the enemies they were about to face. During his expedition into the land he had seen these giants with his own eyes, and the report provided by most members of that expedition exclaimed that all the people there are of great size. They seemed like grasshoppers in our own eyes. Numbers 13:31-33

Defeating such people would be impossible without God's intervention. And this is exactly the message God provided to Joshua just before he went in to claim the land.

The same message and promises God gives us today. What are the *giants* you face in life? What things can get you deeply "discouraged"? God provides the same guidance and comfort to us today that He gave to Joshua.

Many believe that the Old Testament is not relevant in our time. But the Scriptures can't be divided; Christ came to bring us new hope and a way for us personally to come to God, and with His life he demonstrated the reliability of God's love and promises written in the Old Testament.

The tearing of the temple curtain when Christ died is symbolic of this.

> Mark 15:8, "The curtain of the temple was torn in two from top to bottom."

Jesus came to be the sacrifice of the law. No longer was it necessary to kill animals for the forgiveness of sin, but now we can go before God ourselves. The words of God as given to the men in the Old Testament are still for us to hear, to believe and to take into our souls. In many places and in many ways Christ repeated those same promises in His teachings in the New Testament.

> Matthew 28:18-20, "All Authority in heaven and on earth has been given to me. Therefore go and make disciples of all nations, baptizing them in the name of the Father and of the Son and of the Holy Spirit, and teaching them to obey everything I have commanded you. And surely I am with you always, to the very end of the age."

This world is trying to drag us into its clutches, when we are weak it becomes easy to give in to the evils of the world and go back into Satan's grasp. That's when we have to remember the promises given by God and brought to us through Christ. We have Christ with us in the Holy Spirit who is here to guide us and direct us in the path God has for us to travel. We can't give in, we have to remain strong and firm in our belief. When we feel weak we need to pray and ask for His strength to get through the times we are facing. To keep us strong in Him, walking in His light and not giving in to pressures or circumstances; to have the wisdom to make the right decisions for the good of all.

We have been charged to take the word to others, we need to be strong and courageous and wise in our decisions so others can see Christ and not stumble and fall. Sometimes our decisions will not be liked by others, they may not be understood by others, but with God's guidance they are made for the good of all.

Stay strong in Christ and never forget the promise, he will never leave us nor forsake us as long as we are walking in His ways. Always ask for direction from Him in decisions that have to be made. Remember always, God loves you very much and only wants what is best for His kingdom.

Have a great day and God bless!

Trust

Trust in God's care

Good morning:

It seems to me most people allow Satan to use trust to trip them up regarding other people. Even Christians have a difficult time with trust. You hear it all the time, people saying, I can't trust you to do it the way I want it done. Others say, I trust God when it says, you will be with me in eternity. Trust is a big word, it has a lot of meanings, and it is one of those words that can be used as a noun, a verb, or an adjective. What it means depends on how you use it.

As a noun it means:

- A firm belief in the honesty and reliability of another, Faith
- 2) Confident expectation, hope;
- 3) Responsibility resulting from confidence placed in someone
- 4) Care, custody
- 5) Something entrusted to someone

As a verb it means:

- To have confidence in
- To commit (something to the care of another)
- To allow another to do something without misgivings
- To believe, to hope, to expect

As an adjective it means:

- Relating to trust in a person
- Acting as a trustee

There are a lot of ways and things in which Satan can use trust to trip us up, to keep us from the fullness of God. It is easy for Christians to trust God for our salvation and eternity, but when it comes to trusting Him to guide our life, we often fall way short. Satan likes to keep us questioning God about what we should be doing. Are you sure this is what you want for me, or that just doesn't seem like it could be what God wants me to be doing. We can trust Him for His promise that He will save our soul, but we don't have the same trust that He will be able to guide us every moment of every day. We seem to think we have to be in charge of our own daily lives. We use the excuse of, I have been this way my whole life, or that's the way I have always done it. That is Satan, once again, trying to trip us up.

Do you find yourself in that place? Are you attempting to remedy your problems by yourself? It is a mistake to leave God out of your decision-making. Don't spoil the outcome God wants by relying on yourself. Put your trust in Him to guide you. Put your hope in His ability and desire to provide you with the best results. He knows what is right for you, what is right for each situation, for each trial in life.

> Psalm 25; 9-10, "He guides the humble in what is right and teaches them His way. All the ways of the Lord are loving and faithful for those who keep the demands of His covenant."

> Hebrews 2:11-13, "Both the One who makes men holy and those who are made holy are of the same family. So Jesus is not ashamed to call them brothers. He says; I will declare your name to my brothers; in the presence of the congregation I will sing your praises." And again, "I will put my trust in Him," and again He says, "here am I, and the children God has given me."

You can find the same words in Psalm 22:22. The key phrase is *my brothers,* it is seen as coming from the Lord Himself. It is a phrase expressing true dependence on God exemplified in Christ, in His humanity. We, as true believers in Christ, have been given to God through Christ as His brothers and sisters.

We have been given a trust, a responsibility to be like Christ. It is an honor to be trusted by God, we have to fulfill our responsibility and

Kay Ashwell

trust Him to guide our every footstep. Jesus did, if we are His-brothers and sisters we should be able to do the same.

Everything God has done He has done to bring His people back into a personal relationship with Him. He gave us His Son to show us the way to walk and live on this earth, but Jesus referred many times to the Old Testament in His teachings. He left us with the same promises God made to the prophets of old, in Matthew 28: 20b

> Matthew 28b, "..And Surely I am with you always, to the very end of the age."

God never forgets or overlooks His promises. He showed Moses, Joshua, Abraham, and all the rest of the prophets how to trust in Him and in what He told them. Jesus trusted His disciples to carry on the work, the message of salvation, to everyone. He is trusting in us to do the same. We can do no less than trust Him with our very life, our very soul. We need to learn how to trust Him with our everyday living. We need to learn to turn over to Him those worries, those hurts, and those doubts and let Him take care of them. We need to learn to walk in His footsteps. He knows the best way for us to go.

Pray today for God's guidance in everything in your life, at home, at work, and at play. Give it all to Him and let Him show you the best way, the things He wants for you and for your life.

Have a great day and God bless!

Trust in Jesus

Good morning:

Do you feel like you are at the edge of a cliff? Does the gap between you and the other side look like it is far away? Are you down in the ravine with cliffs on both sides and you can't see a way out? The world of today puts us in those places if we are trying to fix things in our life by ourselves. The harder we try the worse things seem to get. The world is in turmoil, the country is in turmoil, governments are out of control and we don't know what tomorrow will bring. You are not alone in feeling that way, but there is a way over to the other side, there is a way out of the ravine.

The nation of Israel, in Jesus time, felt the same way. They were living their lives according to the rules set up by God and the rules set up by man, depending on the country that was in control at the time. They were being told by the Jewish teachers what they could do and when they had to do them, they were being controlled by the Roman government and they were a lost people. They had to do what they were told.

God sent His Son to be the bridge to the other side, to be the ladder for those in the ravine. Many were not prepared for His coming, they didn't recognize Him for who He was. He wasn't the king they thought they were going to get. He wasn't taking them out of this messy life into a new and better one. They only saw Him as a carpenter from Nazareth. So why did God send Him into this world? Why didn't God send another king to lead them out of trouble? How can a God who is limitless in power, wisdom, and love understand what it is like to live life in this world? Does He know how frightening this world can be? Does He understand how raw emotions feel? Does He know pain and the fear of facing death?

> Hebrews 2:14-18;"Since the children have flesh and
> blood, he too shared in their humanity, so that by his

death he might destroy him who holds the power of death, this is the devil, and free those who all their lives were held in slavery by their fear of death. For surely, it is not angels he helps, but Abraham's descendents. For this reason he had to be made like his brothers in every way, in order that he might become a merciful and faithful High Priest in service to God, and that he might make atonement for the sins of the people. Because he himself suffered when he was tempted, he is able to help those who are being tempted."

Jesus' life was not an easy one; He had no place to call His own. Today we would say He was homeless and of low esteem. He lived off the land or off the generosity of those who believed in Him. He lived in this world to show us that we could live in the world and be able to walk obeying God. Jesus came to connect the expanse across the gap. He came to be the ladder out of the ravine. He came to be the bridge between you and God and your humanity. Jesus understands both, and He serves as the perfect mediator for you.

Hebrews 2:10: "In bringing many sons to glory, it was fitting that God, for whom and through whom everything exits, should make the author of their salvation perfect through suffering."

You don't have to stand on that cliff looking over, you don't have to stay in that ravine looking up; you only have to accept God's gifts by coming to Him through the blood of Christ. Recognize your sin, ask for His forgiveness, love Him, love your neighbor, give Him control of your life, and obey the things He calls you to do. Rest in Him and you will find the peace, the understanding, the wisdom to walk in this world and remain in Him.

Jesus is the way to a better life; a happier life, a more peaceful life. You just have to put your trust and faith in Him and follow His ways.

Have a great day and God bless!

Warnings in Hebrews

Hebrews warning 1

Good morning:

In Hebrews there are five warnings for us to acknowledge, the first one is:

> Hebrews 2:1, "We must pay more careful attention, therefore, to what we have heard, so that we do not drift away."

We need to pay closer attention to what is in Scripture, we need to stand firm on what Scripture is telling us we are to be like, what we are to be doing and how we are to be doing it. Sometimes we are put in situations that at first look real good to us, but later we discover there was more there than we were prepared to deal with. In some of these situations we can easily get pulled away from following what Scripture tells us. Some people have their own agenda and will say whatever they need to in order to accomplish that agenda.

We are to follow the example of Christ when it comes to times of decision, not what we have heard. Many people have a good heart and appear to be very stable in their faith, they appear to be knowledgeable about Scripture, and what they say seems to make sense to people. If the people who hear are not grounded in the word, grounded in their faith, able to discern the difference in what they hear and what Scripture says, they become confused. That's how some drift away and others acquire a following that allows them to achieve their agenda. The Pharisee's were able to confuse people because they were the teachers of Scripture. We have the same type of people today. That's why it is so important for believers to be grounded in Scripture.

Many years ago a person who had been attending a Bible study with me for weeks and who I had gone and helped plant spring plants asked me to an evening meeting. I felt comfortable in going as I felt that person believed as I did. It wasn't long after the meeting started I felt God's discerning spirit letting me know it was not a meeting I wanted to be in. I got up and said I don't think I belong here, and I left. When we have God's Spirit in us we need to adhere to what He is telling us.

A grounded Christian who understands what Jesus was teaching is harder to be swayed from their faith. They can stand firm in their knowledge that they are where they need to be with God. That God can use them to help strengthen those who are not as grounded, those who jump from one thing to the next because it sounds good.

Scripture will give us the answers if we take the time to search it out. Answers don't always come in the form we want to hear them. Answers are not always what we want to hear, answers are sometimes difficult to carry out because we know God is calling us to remain in a situation we don't want to remain in, to be a strong link in the recovery process, or for others to learn from. Regardless of how grounded we are, or how sure we are of what Scripture has to say, we are still vulnerable to be swayed from our knowledge by a person who appears to be honest, truthful and a servant of the Lord.

Jesus was always giving us warnings to beware of such situations. To hold firm to what He taught and to ask Him for the strength to deal with each situation in the same way that He would have handled it. What Jesus said was always being questioned by those who had their own agenda. He was always being put to the test of how strong are you? Will you give in and back down, and change what you said. Jesus didn't back down, He didn't give in and give up, He stayed firm in the mission He had, to bring the truth to those who would listen. We have the same mission, when we are put in certain positions or situations, to stand firm in what God has taught us and told us. The world sees enough of things changing with every whim of someone in charge. What they need is to see that there can be stability in the mist of chaos.

There is something to hang onto in times of change. There is a reason to hold firm to the promises of God. God's promises and teachings should be strong enough in a person they can stand firm in the midst of trouble.

Yes, the first warning of Hebrews should cause us to pay attention more closely to what Christ and Scripture says and less on what we hear. Be guided by God and what He has for you to do. If you are listening closely to what He is trying to say to you, it will become clear what you are to do. You may not understand it, you may not really agree with it, but if your heart and not your mind is sure of what is being said to you, you will be able to stand and God can use you for His purpose right where you are.

The strongest thing you can do in uncertain situations is to pray. Pray in faith, believing that through your faith and trust in the Father, you will get the answer you need. Sometimes, when it seems the answers aren't coming, you have to pray with more faith. Sometimes we get impatient for an answer and we miss the answer because we weren't ready to listen. Sometimes our impatience causes us to act before we should. Sometimes it causes us to put ourselves in a position to be vulnerable.

There are things you can do to make sure the temptation to do something which may be out of God's wishes is to:

- Spend time in God's word
- Have extra special times of prayer with Him, listening with your heart and not just your mind
- Avoid putting yourself in a place or situation that makes it difficult to stand your ground.
- Live consistently in public and in private
- Rely on the Holy Spirit for His guidance and direction, not your own or that of someone else.

Be careful, be watchful, that what you hear is what God is saying so that what you hear from others doesn't cause you to be pulled away from what God is telling you. The power of the world is strong, but the power you have in Christ is stronger and when needed will overcome the power of the world.

Have a great day and God bless!

Hebrews warning 2

Good morning:

The second warning in Hebrews:

> Hebrews 3:12, "See to it brothers that none of you has a sinful, unbelieving heart that turns away from the living God." Then if follows with this positive encouragement in verse 13, "But encourage one another daily, as long as it is today, so that none of you may be hardened by sin's deceitfulness."

We can't let this evil world pull us away from our first love, Christ. We are to be with our brothers and sisters in Christ and encourage them and they are to encourage us, and together we can stand firm in our faith. Whether by prayer, by being present with them, by phone or by internet, we are to be an encourager for fellow believers in Christ.

We are to participate in the blessings He has given us with others. We are to hang on to the original confidence we had at our conversion, the faith commitment we made at the time of our conversion; the commitment to follow the ways of God. That includes meeting together with the body of Christ on the Sabbath Day, the day of rest for God's people. The day of rest that He took after creation.

> Genesis 2:1-3, "Thus the heavens and the earth were completed in all their vast array. By the seventh day God had finished the work He had been doing; so on the seventh day He rested from all His work. And God blessed the seventh day and made it Holy, because on it he rested from all the work of creating that He had done."

We have been told to love one another, to stay together, so the devil and the evil world couldn't wear us down and cause us to sin. We are to stand

Kay Ashwell

together, through whatever is thrown at us. We are to make sure our brothers and sisters know when we need something, even if that is just an encouraging word to get through the day. It is easy to stay in touch today with the communications we have. We are not to suffer alone in our moments of stress. We are to let others know. Most of us when something is wrong or there is a crisis, call our family members, we should also call on our Christian family to help us through these times as well. That's what a family is for, to help one another come through whatever it is that we are going through.

We are to help one another not become pulled away, not to become bitter, discouraged, disillusioned, and angry. These are all things that can lead us to become disobedient to the will of God.

> 1 Corinthians 10:13, "No temptation has seized you except what is common to man. And God is faithful; He will not let you be tempted beyond what you can bear. But when you are tempted, He will also provide a way out so that you can stand up under it."

We are all God's workers, when a brother or sister is in a situation that may cause them to stumble and fall we are to come along side them and help hold them up under the stress. Just as Moses' arms were held up by Aaron and Hur when they grew tired at the battle with the Amalekites, we are to hold others up when they became tired, weak or discouraged.

> Exodus 17:12; "When Moses' hands grew tired, they took a stone and put it under him and he sat on it. Aaron and Hur held his hands up, one on one side, one on the other, so that his hands remained steady till sunset".

We are not in physical battles today, but we are in Spiritual battles and we need the strength of other Christians to stand firm and strong.

God knows everything that is going on in our world, in us, and He has told us to stand alongside to hold each other up through these times. Don't try to deal with things on your own, if they seem to become too much to handle, call on your Christian friends and the Christian family to come along side and hold you up. Stay strong in the word and call on God to see you through this time.

> Hebrews 4:12a, "For the word of God is living and active."

Jesus prayed three prayers before his arrest, in the Garden of Gethsemane; this one was for His disciples:

> John 17:6-19, says in part, ".. I am not praying for the world, but for those you have given me, for they are yours. All I have is yours, and all you have is mine. And glory has come to me through them. I will remain in the world no longer, but they are still in the world, and I am coming to you. Holy Father, protect them with the power of your name, the name you gave me, so that they may be one as we are one.....Sanctify them by the truth; your word is truth. As you sent me into the world, I have sent them into the world. For them I sanctify myself, that they too may be truly sanctified."

Read the full chapter of John 17, it is beautiful.

Jesus knew the world would not like us, that we would need each other that is why He said to stay together, to pray together, and to come together in rejoicing. If you don't have Christian friends, I encourage you to get some. Get into a Bible believing Church and find that strength and support that only a true Christian family can give you. If you have Christian friends, stay together, stay strong and be there for each other at all times. Remember, the evil one prowls around trying to find those that He can weaken and turn away. Stay strong in the faith, together.

Have a great day and God bless!

Hebrews warning 3

Good morning:

The third warning in Hebrews is a warning of falling away:

> Hebrews 6: 4-6; "It is impossible for those who have once been enlightened, who have tasted the heavenly gift, who have shared in the Holy Spirit, who have tasted the goodness of the word of God and the powers of the coming age, if they fall away to be brought back to repentance, because to their loss they are crucifying the Son of God all over again and subjecting Him to public disgrace."

This warning is a little harder for some to grasp. There are some basic things you need to understand before its meaning can be clear. First, it is important to understand that when you accepted Christ into your heart you became a Jew, you became like Him. He came from the Israelite Nation that God chose as His family. They were also known as Hebrews. A Hebrew Christian, then, is a person who has accepted God and Christ into their life. Thus all believers are Hebrew Christians. The verse describes what a Christian has learned, they understand what the Scriptures say, they have been shown what the gift of Salvation is, *eternal life* and they have allowed the Holy Spirit to lead and direct them and understand what they will inherit in the coming age, eternal life with Christ.

With this knowledge it becomes easier to understand the warning which is, if you are a true Hebrew Christian and you choose to turn away from the things you know to be true, and you choose to turn your back on those teachings, you will not be able to receive the blessings of repentance, because by making that choice you are putting Jesus' life in question. If you turn your back on your Christian faith and willing choose to go against what you have learned you are saying that Jesus' death on the cross has no meaning for you.

Let's get one thing straight, however, this is not saying if you are tempted and sin that you can't receive forgiveness. God knows we all sin and when we recognize that sin we can go to Him and confess it and He will forgive us. This is talking about someone who says I am no longer going to believe that God can do anything for me. They totally turn their back on God and become one with the world. They totally turn away from Christ.

The next 2 verses give you a better idea of this if you put yourself in the place of the word land.

> Hebrews6: 7-8, "Land that drinks in the rain often falling on it and that produces a crop useful to those for whom it is farmed receives the blessings of God. But land that produces thorns and thistles is worthless and is in danger of being cursed. In the end it will be burned."

In other words, those who welcome the Scriptures and the teachings and go on and help others come to Him will receive His blessings, but those who don't follow or turn from it and let bad things enter into and become the focal point of their life will not receive the blessing.

In the same sense, a Christian is to grow in the knowledge and understanding of Christ. They cannot continue to just believe; they have to grow and become a useful servant of God and allow Him to use them for the purposes He sees fit. In other words you cannot just believe and do nothing for the kingdom and receive the full blessings of God. When you are His you become a part of a large family that works together to show Christ to the world so the world knows there is a better way to live.

A true believer will hear what God is asking them to do and will become a part of His family by participating and learning and growing each day, being willing to help their neighbor, regardless of the circumstances. To walk with the love that has been given them, by sharing with others the blessings God has given to them.

A Christian cannot become stagnant; they have to be alive with the love of God and the truth of the Scriptures. They have to be showing those things to the world. They need to be participating regularly with other Christian brothers and sisters to remain strong and vital. They need to be in prayer daily, they need to be in the word daily, and they need to be willing to serve others as Christ did.

Let your light shine before man so that they can see the blessings God gives to those who believe in Him. Turn away from the things of the world and concentrate on the things of God. The day will come when you will be rewarded for your faithfulness to Him. Don't turn your back on Him or He will turn His back on you.

Have a great day and God bless!

Hebrews warning 4

Good morning:

The fourth warning in Hebrews is:

> Hebrews 10:26, "If we deliberately keep on sinning after we have received the knowledge of the truth no sacrifice for sins is Left; but only a fearful expectation of judgment and of raging fire that will consume the enemies of God."

This particular warning is for those who after receiving the truth of God, understanding its significance, and having been involved with worshiping with other Christians, turns and rejects those teachings and starts to sin, knowing the consequences. They deliberately sin, turning away from the Christian faith, which they once claimed.

That is a state of sinning that cannot be reversed. There is no sacrifice for these sins left. In the Old Testament, Numbers gives a sacrifice for unintentional sin.

> Numbers: 15:30-31, "But anyone who sins defiantly, whether native-born or alien, blasphemes the Lord, and that person must be cut off from his people. Because he has despised the Lord's word and broken his commands, that person must surely be cut off: his guilt remains on him."

The native-born is an Israelite; the alien is any other that has joined them.

What a terrible place to be. To know the living God and know what He went through for each of us on the cross, and to know what He has promised us for our future, and then turn your back on it. To give up

Kay Ashwell

that grace and peace and love for selfish desires, personal gain, a piece of what the world offers. Would it be worth it?

I pray your answer is a loud no, nothing could turn me from the love and peace and contentment I know as one of His children. Yes, we will all sin, but that is unintentional sin and we can be forgiven for that just by recognizing it as sin and asking for His forgiveness. But to give that up, to have to carry all the sin and guilt on yourself, doesn't make a lot of sense to me. But there are those who do that, just for a taste of what the world is offering them. That's what this warning is, don't turn your back on God.

A better place to be:

> Hebrews 10: 19-25, "Therefore, brothers, since we have confidence to enter the Most Holy Place by the blood of Jesus, by a new and living way opened for us through the curtain, that is, His body, and since we have a great priest over the house of God, let us draw near to God with a sincere heart in full assurance of faith, having our hearts sprinkled to cleanse us from a guilty conscience, and having our bodies washed with pure water. Let us hold unswerving to the hope we profess, for He who promised is faithful. And let us consider how we may spur one another on toward love and good deeds. Let us not give up meeting together, as some are in the habit of doing. But let us encourage one another-and all the more as you see the Day approaching."

For those who may not understand the phrase, opened for us through the curtain, on the day Christ was crucified, at the moment of His death, the huge curtain that separated the inner temple, where only the high priests were allowed from the outer temple, where the people were gathered, was torn from top to bottom, signifying there was no need for anyone to intercede on our behalf. We could talk to God ourselves, we could ask Him for His forgiveness and mercy when we sin. This is what separates the old law from the new law of God. There is no more shedding of animal blood to atone for our sin, Christ took that upon Himself on the cross, once and for all. There is no need for someone else to intercede on our behalf. Now we can go to God ourselves. We can have a personal relationship with Him.

We are to remain strong together; we are to encourage each other when the world would like to isolate us. We are to look expectantly toward the Day when He will call His people out of this world to wait with Him while Satan has his way here on earth. For those who don't come to believe until that time, the world will not be a nice place to try and survive in. Have yourself and your loved ones ready for that Day. Ask God into your heart, follow His teachings, get into a church of believers, and get your children in one also. I don't want any of you to have to suffer the coming years of tribulation here on earth.

Hold onto your faith, stand firm together, and stay in the word and you will not have to worry about this fourth warning. Be aware of it and try to keep any you know and love from falling into this sin. Remember to walk one day at a time with your hand in His is the ultimate goal. There is no yesterday and there is no tomorrow, there is only today. Live it the way the Lord asks you to live it.

Have a great day and God bless!

Hebrews warning 5

Good morning:

The fifth and final warning:

> Hebrews; 12:25, "See to it that you do not refuse Him who speaks. If they did not escape when they refused Him who warned them on earth, how much less will we, if we turn away from Him who warns us from heaven. At that time his voice shook the earth, but now he has promised, Once more I will shake not only the earth but also the heavens. The words once more indicate the removing of what can be shaken—that is, created things—so that what cannot be shaken will remain. Therefore, since we are receiving a kingdom that cannot be shaken, let us be thankful, and so worship God acceptably with reverence and awe, for our God is a consuming fire."

We are not to turn away from God when He calls to us. Some people have had Him call to them on many occasions and they continue to ignore His call. They refuse to let Him come into their life and be a part of His family. God is offering us a place in a kingdom that cannot be shaken. Christ offered us the way to enter that kingdom. If those who are called continue to ignore the call to accept the heavenly kingdom they will be cut off.

God warned the nation of Israel not to ignore His commands. Jesus warned those on earth not to ignore the gift the Father was offering, and in Revelation it warns us what will happen when we try to live in both heaven and earth. It can't be done. We have to make a choice to live for Him and receive the blessings that await us in His Kingdom or we choose to live in the world with all its evil and ugliness. It's easiest to live in the world and many will remain in it. Many will ignore this warning. But for those who choose to hear and listen and obey the Father, a better life awaits them. He is waiting to show them the riches they will inherit as a son or daughter of the King.

The road to His kingdom is harder to travel, but the rewards are greater. Going on into Hebrews chapter 13 we find out what we are to do and how we are to continue in holding firm to what we have learned.

> Hebrews: 13: 1- 6, "Keep on loving each other as brothers. Do not forget to entertain strangers, for by so doing some people have entertained angels without knowing it. Remember those in prison as if you were their fellow prisoners, and those who are mistreated as if you yourselves were suffering. Marriage should be honored by all and the marriage bed kept pure, for God will judge the adulterer and all the sexually immoral. Keep your lives free from the love of money and be content with what you have, because God has said, 'never will I leave you; never will I forsake you.' So we say with confidence, The Lord is my helper, I will not be afraid. What can man do to me"?

It goes on to say to follow our leaders, it is talking about Christian leaders, Christian principles, which are given to us by leaders who are following the commands of God. Many other worldly, and even so-called Christian leaders, will pull us away from His kingdom to suffer in theirs.

There are warnings and there are promises in Hebrews. The warnings are to not ignore the salvation or give up the pursuit of Holiness. If we do we will face the judgment of God just as the rebellious Israelites did in the desert. It tells us to follow Jesus faithfully and with perseverance, having confidence to enter the Sanctuary of God. We are to preserve the faith as Jesus taught us and we are to encourage each other in the face of hardships. We are to pursue living a holy life and to assist in carrying out the will of the Father.

Kay Ashwell

The last of the book is a prayer:

> Hebrews: 13:20-21, "May the God of peace, who through the blood of the eternal covenant brought back from the dead our Lord Jesus, that great Shepherd of the sheep, equip you with everything good for doing His will, and may He work in us what is pleasing to Him, through Jesus Christ, to whom be glory forever and ever. Amen."

Stand firm, do not stray, and stay in the loving care of the Father until the end. Depend on and call on brothers and sisters in Christ to help you over the rough spots and the down times that will surely come into each life. The hope is that there is a better way, a final resting place with our Lord in His kingdom which will prevail over this evil world. The warnings are strong, but time is short and we must not waver in our faith for a moment, Satan is just waiting to bring us down. We must not give in to this world. We must continue to do the work and be the people He has taught us to be. Our reward will be in eternity with Him.

Have a great day and God bless!

Tests and Trials

Tests and Trials make us strong

Good morning:

A month ago our granddaughter got herself into a situation which caused several to worry about her. She had accepted Jesus as her savior, but had not followed through with getting into a church. After talking to her and realizing she was being tempted to be lead away from who she really was, her grandpa and I prayed with her over the phone and encouraged her to stop seeing those people and to start going to church. We explained that temptations come every day to each of us and it is up to us to either reject them or to go with them.

Those temptations come even to Christians every day but because we have Jesus as our savior, who has gone through the temptations of the world, we can ask Him to help us through them. To Christians, temptations are an opportunity to experience success in turning Satan away.

> 1 Corinthians 10:12-13, "So if you think you are standing firm, be careful that you don't fall. No temptation has seized you except what is common to man. And God is faithful; he will not let you be tempted beyond what you can bear. But when you are tempted, he will also provide a way out so that you can stand up under it."

These tests can make us stronger if we seek God and take the way out He gives us. I believe we all need to be encouraged to find positive solutions to our temptations each day. We never know when one little word, one offer of prayer with someone, one hug, one smile at a stranger, one phone call to someone who is on our mind can change that person's life and attitude. It's easy to ignore these things, the world doesn't do them, it wants to keep people in a negative attitude all the time, that's how Satan works, but a smile at someone who has stepped in front of you in a line, who has said a negative word because you were in their way, can change that person's attitude.

People need to see the joy we have in knowing our Lord, they need to feel that there is a better way to live. Jesus was constantly given negative things to deal with; He showed us how to overcome them. As Christians we have the resources to overcome what the world throws at us. We just have to ask and Christ is there and will show us what to do.

It goes along with praying without ceasing, when temptations or testing is in our path we just have to say, ok Lord what would you have me do with this? We need to look for the positive in everything we come in contact with or do during the day.

> 1 Peter 5:7 says, "Cast all your anxiety on him because he cares for you."

He cares what happens to each of us, and He cares for that person who we are in touch with, or have just met; what would He have us do to help that person? I think we sometimes forget that God wants us to show love, joy, peace, and kindness to everyone we see or meet or have any interaction with. When we are slow to react to a negative and when we trust Him to turn a negative into a positive we are showing others the things He has given us. When we are positive things around us are positive, negative breeds negative but positive will produce positive.

I think we need to remember what David said in Psalm 85:

> Psalm 86:15, "But You, O Lord, are a compassionate and gracious God, slow to anger and abounding in love and faithfulness."

Let's wrap ourselves in the armor of God, let's face each day with positive love, joy, and peace in our hearts and minds and go out there and let others around us see there is a positive way out of temptations, trials, tests and just plain everyday survival.

God bless and have a great day!

Tests and Trials will purify us

Good morning:

You hear many people talking about where we are in the end times. Many don't understand them, many don't think about them and many don't believe in them. However, for those who believe in them the signs are very strong that we are probably entering the beginning of the end. How long will it last? No one can say. What we do know is that as bad as it is now, it will get worse. Christians who believe in Christ will suffer for their faith. These times are for the testing of our faith. God is judging His people. Testing them to see which of them is a true Son or Daughter of His.

> 1 Peter 4:12-19, "Dear friends, do not be surprised at the painful trial you are suffering as though something strange were happening to you. But rejoice that you participate in the sufferings of Christ, so that you may be overjoyed when His glory is revealed. If you are insulted because of the name of Christ, you are blessed, for the Spirit of glory and of God rests on you. If you suffer, it should not be as a murderer or thief, or any other kind of criminal, or even as a meddler. However, if you suffer as a Christian, do not be ashamed, but praise God that you bear that name. For it is time for judgment to begin with the family of God, and if it begins with us, what will the outcome be for those who do not obey the gospel of God? And, if it is hard for the righteous to be saved, what will become of the ungodly and the sinner? So then, those who suffer according to God's will should commit themselves to their faithful Creator and continue to do well."

The trials, tests, and suffering we go through in Christ's name are to purify and strengthen us for the day when we have to stand firm in our faith for Him. There will be no room for maybes, we will only be able to stand for Him or against Him. The world won't accept a maybe, a fence sitter. In the end, you will have to make a choice and that choice won't be an easy one to walk. But it is the only one that will get you into His kingdom to live with Him forever.

Peter wrote those words, something for us to hold onto, something to help us through these times of trials, and sufferings which are to come.

> 1 Peter 4:7-11, "The end of all things is near. Therefore be clear minded and self-controlled so that you can pray. Above all, love each other deeply, because love covers over a multitude of sins. Offer hospitality to one another without grumbling. Each one should use whatever gift he has received to serve others, faithfully administering God's grace in its various forms. If anyone speaks, he should do it as one speaking the very words of God. If anyone serves, he should do it with the strength God provides, so that in all things God may be praised through Jesus Christ. To Him be the glory and the power forever and ever. Amen."

Everyone will have to give an account to God for the life they have lived. Peter tells us this is the reason the gospel was given to us, to show us the way. Christ lived and walked this earth to show man the way to live; He was crucified for this life. He went to the cross willingly for each and every person in the world, then and now. It was for the living and the dead, for those not even born yet. It was given for all mankind until He comes again to reign in a perfect world.

As His children, as brothers or sisters to Christ, we have an obligation to live the life He sets before us. The life He planned for us to have before we were born. We have responsibilities, gifts, talents, to be used the way and for the reason He gave them to us. Some have more than one gift, because He knows they can use them for Him. Don't struggle with the gift, or talent or responsibility you have been given. Use it for His glory where He leads you to use it. If you suffer for it, use it anyway, the way He directs you to use it.

We have a responsibility to lead others to Him, we have a responsibility to care for each other, and we have a responsibility to let His love shine through each and every one of us in everything we do and say.

Have a great day and God bless!

.

Tests and Trials will bring peace

Good morning:

Is your faith being tested these days? Mine is! I think of Job when life starts to press in on me. The testing he went through is far more than the testing I go through. No matter what he went through he maintained his belief in God and in the end came out with far more blessings. God tests each of us, how we respond to that testing determines the outcome. If we are faithful and carry on through all of them with the right heart and mind in the end we will have more blessings come from them than can be imagined.

We are tested in one way or another every day. We may not even know we are being tested, but we are.

> Psalm 26:2-3: "Test me, O Lord, and try me, examine
> my heart and my mind; for your love is ever before me,
> and I walk continually in your truth."

We all test things ourselves, to make sure they are secure and true. We test things, and we are tested by others every day. How we respond and how we react to them is what matters. Not the testing itself. We make knots, test them to make sure they will hold, we test the truth about what is told to us, by finding out the facts, we test the love of others by the way they respond in different situations. We are being tested all the time, conscious of it or not, it makes us stronger, to make us surer of our walk, to let us see we cannot.walk this life without Him as our guide.

Being tested is good for us, good for our faith, but it is sometimes tough to go through. Sometimes, like Job, many things come at us all at once. Those are times when our faith is being tested the most. How will we deal with it, how will we respond to it, is our faith strong enough to carry us through?

We find Job answering friends' questions and he has this to say:

Job 22: 21-22; "Submit to God and be at peace with Him; in this way prosperity will come to you. Accept instruction from His mouth and lay up His words in your heart."

Job 23:10-11, "But He knows the way that I take; when He has tested me; I will come forth as gold. My feet have closely followed His steps; I have kept to His way without turning aside."

For myself I pray that the testing I go through, the way I respond to it, the faith I have will bring Glory to my Lord.

2 Corinthians 4:6; "For God, who said, let light shine out of darkness, made his light shine in our hearts to give us the light of the knowledge of the glory of God in the face of Christ."

2 Corinthians 4:8-10 & 16-18; "We are hard pressed on every side, but not crushed; perplexed, but not in despair; persecuted, but not abandoned, struck down, but not destroyed. We always carry around in our body the death of Jesus, so that the life of Jesus may also be revealed in our body."......"Therefore we do not lose heart. Though outwardly we are wasting away, yet inwardly we are being renewed day by day; for our light and momentary troubles are achieving for us an eternal glory that far outweighs them all. So we fix our eyes not on what is seen, but on what is unseen. For what is seen is temporary, but what is unseen is eternal."

Whatever test I am going through, whatever test He puts in front of me, I pray it's over soon. And I hope I'll pass the test and that I'll come out of it stronger, wiser, and closer to Him. Sometimes it's hard to see the end, sometimes I may get discouraged and stressed, but all I have to do is reach out and say, Please, God, help me!!

Have a great day and God bless!

Conclusion

I pray that you have gained strength and hope and understanding from this book. I believe God has an overall message throughout. One that will bring assurance, peace and perseverance to Christians.

There are two messages which God keeps giving me; first for those who call themselves Christians, it's time to get Hot for God.

> Revelations 2: 4-5; "You have forsaken your first love. Remember the height from which you have fallen! Repent and do the things you did at first."

> Revelation 3:15-16 "I know your deeds, that you are neither cold nor hot. I wish you were either one or the other! So because you are lukewarm – neither hot nor cold – I am about to spit you out of my mouth."

Second for those who haven't made a decision to let God into their lives; Jesus from the beginning of His ministry taught:

> Matthew 4:17b; "Repent for the kingdom of heaven is at hand."

It's necessary to recognize your sin and ask God for the gift of his forgiveness found through Jesus.

> Matthew 7: 7-8, "ask and it will be given to you, seek and you will find; knock and the door will be opened to you. For everyone who asks receives; he who seeks finds; and to him who knocks, the door will be opened."

> Acts 2: 38; "Repent and be baptized, every one of you, in the name of Jesus Christ for the forgiveness of your sins. And you will receive the gift of the Holy Spirit."

God wants all to become a part of His kingdom. Now is the time to make a decision, the time is getting short; don't put it off. We don't know what the next minute may bring.

You just need to say a prayer asking God to forgive your sins;
You need to ask him into your heart knowing Jesus is the Savior of the world.
You have to believe He sent His only Son, Jesus, to earth to die on the cross for each of us;
That He arose from death, giving us an opportunity to be with him in eternity.
If you sincerely believe and ask you will become one of God's children and join with other brothers and sisters in carrying the message of love, peace, and hope to others in need.

God bless each of you!

About the Author

I was born in Park Rapids, Minn. in 1941, I was the first born to two wonderful parents. A sister and 2 brothers followed. We moved from Minn. to Idaho Falls, Id. in the winter of 1947, where I lived until I married my first husband. We had 4 children 2 boys and 2 girls. I moved to North Idaho in 1972 where my children all graduated from high school.

I married Don in 1983. We moved to Wyoming in 1984 with his job where we both were volunteer firefighter, EMT's until 1990 when we moved back to North Idaho. We were instrumental in starting the Nazarene Church in Bonners Ferry, Idaho.

Don was injured at work in 2002 and he retired and we got an RV and found ourselves in South East Texas. We started working with a small church and God kept us there serving Him until 2018 when I brought Don back to Idaho and the children. He had fast moving Dementia and needed to be near the children.

While in Texas God saw me through a Hip replacement in 2010 and a rare cancer in 2016. I served as Adult Sunday School teacher and Education chairman for many years at the church in Texas. God has used me in many ways throughout my life. At 79 He still uses me and gives me new things to do. This book being one of them.

There are several step children with many grand kids. We have many, many grandchildren and many more great grandchildren.

This year God called Don Home to spend Eternity with Him, March 14, 2020.

In my introduction to this book it relates how the book came about and other details about my life.

Kay Ashwell

Printed in the United States
By Bookmasters